The
7Myths
about
LOVE
... Actually!

First published by O Books, 2010

O Books is an imprint of John Hunt Publishing Ltd.,
The Bothy, Deershot Lodge, Park Lane, Ropley, Hants, SO24 OBE, UK
office1@o-books.net . www.o-books.net

Distribution in:
US/Canada: NBN (National Book Network)
Tel: 1 800 462 6420 Fax: 1 800 338 4550
Email: custserv@nbnbooks.com
15200 NBN Way, Blue Ridge Summit, PA 17214 USA

UK & Europe: Orca Book Services Ltd
For home trade orders: tradeorders@orcabookservices.co.uk
Tel: 01235 465521 Fax 01235 465555
For export trade orders: exportorders@orcabookservices.co.uk
Tel: 01235 465516 Fax 01235 465555
Individual orders: directorders@orcabookservices.co.uk
Tel: 01235 465577 Fax 01235 465556
Orders by post: 160 Milton Park, Abingdon, Oxon OX14 4SD

Australia & New Zealand: Brumby Books
Tel: 61 3 9761 5535 Fax: 61 3 9761 7095
Email: sales@brumbybooks.com.au   website: www.brumbybooks.com.au
10 Southfork Drive, Kilsyth South, Victoria, Australia 3137

Singapore, Malaysia, Thailand, Hong Kong & Taiwan:
Pansing Distribution Pte Ltd
Tel: (65) 6319 9939 Fax: (65) 6462 5761
Email: kemal@pansing.com
438 Ang Mo Kio Ave 10; Ang Mo Kio Industrial Park 1
Singapore 569619

South Africa: Stephan Phillips (pty) Ltd
Email: orders@stephanphillips.com
Tel: 27 21 4489839 Telefax: 27 21 4479879
Old Castle Brewery, 6 Beach Road, Woodstock 7925, SA

Text copyright © Mike George 2010

Cover Design: Arati Devasher
Page Layout and Typesetting: Arati Devasher, www.aratidevasher.com

ISBN - 978-1-84694-288-4

A CIP catalogue record for this book is available from the British Library.

Printed in the UK by Printondemand-worldwide.com
Printed in the US by Arvato Digital Print Services

The 7Myths about LOVE ... Actually!

The Journey from your Head to the Heart of your Soul

Mike George

BOOKS

CLEAR THINKING

This is the first in a series of Clear Thinking books. Clear Thinking is a weekly e-article that currently circulates to around 15,000 people worldwide. Topics vary each week. They all serve to sustain your ongoing learning and unlearning in the territory self-awareness and the reawakening to what is true within you. While the material in this book is new, future Clear Thinking books will include many of the articles that have appeared over the last four years.

Feedback to Clear Thinking

"I would just wish to thank you for all the content you share and make available to everyone. 'Clear Thinking' is always embraced heartily every week. Your website is also a beautiful haven for people to visit"

—Ewan Findlay

"I have been receiving your articles for quite some time now and have sometimes thought that I have heard all you have to say. But each time a new CT arrives in my inbox, I find I am continually learning to think differently. Your recent article on 'Being Centred' has blown me away. Suddenly I am free!"

—Christine Breddy

"Mike, I love your messages. They are elegant, honest and from the heart."

—Laurie Attwood

"Thank you Mike, I so enjoy reading Clear Thinking. It often feels as if you are writing just for me, as if you know what I need in this moment. I was mentioning Clear Thinking to a few friends who also subscribe and they all felt the same way about it."

—Dermot Fitzpatrick

"Love your weekly Clear Thinking articles! Great insights for which I send you my compliments because it is not always easy to explain such a shifts in perspective"

—Vera Kamphuis

If you would like to subscribe, please go to
www.relax7.com and then to Room 1. It's free.

Dedication

To all who seek
love in their relationships
peace in their hearts
and happiness in their life
and who have not yet realized
that 'they' are already there.

Questions or Comments

If you have any questions or comments regarding the ideas and
insights in this book please talk to me at mike@relax7.com

For further insights, articles, meditations and retreats visit

www.mythsoflove.com
www.relax7.com

 Contents

The Jewel in the Crown

In our search for love we will look in almost every corner of the world. We seek love as acceptance and approval in our many relationships. We desire the ideal love in the fiction of the perfect romance. We expect to find love in what we do, what we acquire and even in the places we go. There are always temporary satisfactions on these roads, but disappointment is also inevitable, until we realize they are deadends.

It may take us a little time to realize that the jewel in the crown of the human spirit cannot be found anywhere but in our own heart. It was, is and always will be there, which is 'here'!

To search for love is to avoid love. And yet how are we to know this when the habit of searching is so deep and, in many ways, a perverted comfort in itself. How are we to know love, when we continue to mistakenly believe that we need to acquire it, earn it or even win it? Intuitively we know that it is only by opening our own heart and in the giving of our self, without condition, that love can start to flow into and through our life.

Only by acts of selfless kindness, unconditional forgiveness and limitless compassion is love felt. Only by the intention to benefit 'the other' before the self, is love made real and realized. And yet, even this is only possible when it is not a deliberated act, when motive is innocent. The motivation 'to love' is not love, for love needs no motive.

It is the satisfaction of all need. When love is realized, there are no needs. In 'reality', there never was.

Only when we can bring an end to wanting, taking, keeping and even giving in the 'name' of love, is the jewel in the crown able to shine again. And when its light is seen it is found to be in the place where it cannot be sought and can never leave, which is *here*, and in the only time it can ever exist, which is *now*.

In that moment, all the accumulated mythologies of love fall away. In that moment the words most used in the affairs of humankind, "I love you," are transformed from an illusion into something closer to the truth, "I am love for you." And then into the deepest truth that words are inadequate to describe, "I am love."

And then on to the final enlightenment, free from the need to describe, free of all concepts, simply "I am."

And even then, beyond enlightenment, into the 'silence of being', a silence that both embraces and enjoins all and everything.

Such is the nature of love.

It is what 'I am' and it is what 'you are'.

It is us.

IT is.

Introduction

To 'speak' about love is to speak about what you are. To 'live' as love is to be your self. To 'do' love is to create an expression of what you are according to the situation you are in and whoever may be in front of you. There are not different 'types' of love, there is only one love, but there are many faces and forms of love as it finds its way through us all and out into the world. Compassion, care, respect, forgiveness are only a few of the almost infinite ways that the light of love can be felt, seen and known.

I never knew all this. No one taught me any of this. And the vast majority of us seem to be unaware of this. Which is probably why the world is now a place filled with so many conflicted relationships and so many unhappy people. It explains why the simplest definition of 'stress' is the *absence of love in relationship,* and why life and living can be an equally miserable experience for those who apparently 'have everything' as it can be for those who 'have nothing'. Happiness is impossible without love. Not the love 'for' something and not even the love 'of' someone. Just the 'presence' of love ...actually!

If only I had known this when I was knee high to a grasshopper. If only my largely wasted time in school had just the smallest input into the true meaning of love. If only my responsible, dedicated, kind and hard working parents had been able to pass on some wisdom about the very essence of life. If only! But they didn't. They couldn't. They too were as unaware as so many others are about the true meaning of love.

So here we go. A book about love. Please don't expect a relationship manual, or a treatise on how to find the perfect lover, or indeed how to fall in love. To bring love to those levels only sustains our limited understanding about love. This is more an investigation as to why love is so frequently absent, avoided or simply misunderstood, both in the microcosm of a personal relationship and in the macrocosm of life itself. In the process we may catch a glimpse of the truth about love as we realize that what we think is love is something almost entirely different. There is only one small challenge. Words are not enough. Words get in the way of knowing love. They cloud the territory of the heart. The language of words is by nature dualistic. Love, however, is beyond opposites. Ultimately love has no opposite. It is the very fabric that holds together all that exists at all levels. Love is like an invisible matrix that connects everything and everyone. Even when it appears that things, people and even our own minds, are separated and falling apart, the light of love is ever present in the background. Words can never come close to love, which is why all spiritual texts concerned with love can only signpost the way, can only point in the direction where you may see, realize and come to know love for your self.

This is why there is also an inherent contradiction in writing about love, especially a book with the subtitle that indicates a 'journey from head to heart'. Books, or more precisely words and sentences, are ideas and concepts that come from the head and can only live in the head, as thoughts. At best they can point to the heart, the inner world of awareness and feelings, but they can never go there. Just as the word 'water' has never made you wet, so the word 'love' can never make you know, feel or realise love is what you are.

While what happens in your head can be an expression of your heart, you will have to leave your head to return to your heart. Which basically means you'll have to go beyond 'thinking about' love to know love and be love... again.

Loss of Meaning

Ask a room full of people to define love and it's likely you'll gather just as many definitions as there are people in the room. Love is probably one of the most used, misused and abused words in our language. This is also why, while it may be easy to 'talk the talk of love', it's far from easy to 'walk the walk' of love'.

The main reason why we share a common ignorance around the meaning of love, and a stunted ability to walk the walk, is not solely due to its elusiveness in terms of words, ideas and concepts. It's more to do with our common loss of self identity and self awareness. Or more accurately, our tendency to invest our identity in something that we are not.

For many, this will not be a new idea, however you may not have noticed the subtleties of this habit. For others, this will be a new insight and possibly a revelation once it's fully seen. But until you clearly see and understand the process by which you habitually lose your sense of self in some thing that you are not, you will never know true love.

Another factor that has contributed to love's apparent disappearance from daily life is modern entertainment. It is in this context that love has been decimated, both by the mythology of romance and the glorification of material achievement. From children's fairy stories to the famed Mills and Boon tales of romance, to Hollywood's glamorous representations of success and happiness, the idea of love has been squeezed, confined and limited.

The commercialization of the belief that love can only be found through personal achievement, the acquisition of products or in an exclusive relationship, only makes love small, elusive and distant when, in truth, it is unlimited, huge and instantly accessible. This manipulation of the meaning of love also keeps us focused on an external search. Looking for love 'out there' only delays the discovery of love and blocks the entry of love into our life, when, in truth, it already lives in the last place we learn to look, in our own heart. In Part I we explore why we are so confused and distracted by the mythology that has grown around the idea of love!

Don't Believe a Word

There is of course only one barrier to the rediscovery and realisation of the jewel in the crown of the human spirit, and that is our oldest and dearest companion - the ego. When you understand the ego you begin to understand almost everything. However, that understanding is only possible when you see for yourself how you create the ego within your self. If you study the ego academically through the eyes of the so-called experts you will likely become confused by concepts. But if you can see how you create your ego you will stand at the threshold of true freedom and the authentic happiness that accompanies that freedom.

If you already have some 'learned concepts' about ego I would recommend that you put them on temporary hold and shift them into a storage cupboard within your consciousness. People like Sigmund Freud and Carl Jung left us with a wonderful legacy of work, including their concepts of ego, the superego and the id etc. Their ideas underpin many schools of psychology and psychiatry. But you don't need to know all that. They are more likely to get in the way. When we arrive at the ego in Part II, I recommend you don't believe a word that you read, however don't not believe either, but see if you can see what I describe for your self, in your self, about your self. I know it is possible to do so – it only depends on how interested you are, and how willing you are to give your self some time in self-reflection, contemplation and meditation. When you 'see for your self', instead of just believing others, you then become the authority in your own life, you become the master of your consciousness again. Which is as it should be.

One Self, One I, One YOU

I am assuming that you are aware that you are not your body, that you know (in theory at least) that you are the being of consciousness that animates the form that you occupy.

Sometimes it's called spirit, or the soul, or the authentic self. Even if you have not fully realized your self as the intangible, invisible, infinite energy of the 'I' that says 'I Am', you at least understand the idea. If you do, you may also realize that the subtitle on the front cover is not quite accurate. It states *the journey from your head to the heart of your soul*, implying that they are separate 'components' or aspects of you.

In reality, head, heart and soul are all one. They are all you. **Head** just means the function of thinking, the creation of thought, which is what you 'do' within your consciousness, which is also you! **Heart** is not your physical heart, but the heart of your consciousness which is you. **Soul** is you again, because you don't have a soul – you are a soul! There isn't some mysterious spirit lurking somewhere in your body. You're it! The primary reason we tend to think too much and both block and distort the energy of our heart, is self-forgetfulness. As the book progresses you will begin to see more clearly how you have been brilliantly taught how not to be your self. You are reading this book because you are either consciously or unconsciously searching for your authentic self. In Part III we connect your search for your self with your search for happiness and see why they are one and the same.

I recommend you take your time, read slowly, contemplate much, meditate often and reflect frequently upon what you read. As you do you may begin to see why you are not being your self, why you are not feeling your self, why you are a little confused about your self, and why this 'thing called love' seems so elusive to your self. It is a universal condition.

If you have any questions or require clarification on any of the ideas and insights please feel free to connect and share what is unclear and e-mail me at **mike@relax7.com**

Bon Voyage!

Part ONE

A
LOVE
Story

This is a story about YOUR heart.
It's what you could call the 'real' Toy Story!
But remember, it's just a story.

Are you sitting comfortably?

In the beginning
your love was innocent and then...

Once upon a time, when you were still very young, you received your first toy from big people. You were encouraged to play with your toy and you were expected by those big people to be happy when you played with your toy. And while you were happy with your new toy, you were even happier when you saw that they were happy that you were happy. The more you loved your toy, the more the big people, who gave you the toy loved you. Or so it seemed. Gradually you learned that happiness and love were dependent on acquiring and playing with toys, and letting the big people know you were happy and that you loved them more for making you happy.

Then one dark and predestined day, you had your first earth-shattering experience. Someone broke your toy. You screamed and cried and, for the first time, you knew the pain of sorrow. Your heart broke, briefly. Your heart had become attached to the toy and, when the toy was broken, it seemed like your heart was also *broken.*

Of course your heart didn't break literally, but metaphorically, and you created your first experience of suffering. You also succumbed to the illusion that the person who broke your toy was the same person who broke your heart, and was therefore the creator of your suffering. Since that moment it's been downhill all the way.

Selfish becomes natural

This first experience of pain, which you thought was caused by someone else, triggered your decision to try to protect yourself from a recurrence. So you began to protect your toys. No-one else was allowed to play with your toys, especially with your favourite toys. This was then interpreted by the big people, who gave you your toys, as 'selfish'. And while it was obviously a negative judgment of you, they seemed resigned to the emergence of your selfish nature, as if it were ... natural. You learned to believe that being selfish was OK. And as you built an imaginary fence around your toys, you didn't realize you were really building a wall around your heart. This began to diminish the natural emanation of the energy of your heart, often referred to as love. Your heart was becoming *blocked*.

While you allowed new toys to come 'over the wall', you began to keep other people, those breakers of toys, at a distance, just beyond the wall. Occasionally you would let someone in, or you might come out and let your heart shine all over a new person in your life (as if they were a toy).

Once again however, they would do something unexpected, something which contradicted an image of how you wanted them to be, an image to which your heart had become attached. With your heart invested in your expectation of them, once again you suffered and the illusion, that other people were the cause of your suffering, became stronger and deeper.

So one day, just to be on the safe side, you decided to completely isolate some parts of your heart altogether. This served to completely deny the sunshine of your love, to a few others at first and many others later. Slowly but surely, your heart began to *freeze* over.

Life without love

Little did you realize that, as you blocked the sunshine of your heart to others, you were doing the same to yourself. Instead of radiating an unconditioned love to those around you, you began to give love to some people a little, to others more and a few not at all. Being completely ignorant of your self as the first source of love to your self, you did not realize that, as you denied your love (your self) to others, you were really denying your self (your love) to your self! Like a lake that becomes a desert without rain, like a tree that withers without water, your heart *withered* without the nourishing flow of your own love.

By now your heart is broken, blocked, frozen and withered. But you were just getting started! As you watched those around you, especially those big people who brought you your first toys, it seemed they had found love and happiness in life in other more interesting ways. As you became bewitched by the technicolour, multi-channel, multicultural electronic window onto 'life as entertainment', you learned to believe that love, and therefore happiness, could be gained from others, either through your looks, your status, your personality or your achievements.

And so the external searching and striving for love, in the form of others' recognition and approval, began in many areas of your life. You began to search in your work, in the acquisition of objects, in your relationships with others, in your achievements and even in your family, for something or someone to restore love to your heart and so bring happiness to your life.

You were occasionally able to dull the pain of your aching heart, but it was always only temporary, and you succeeded only in creating a feeling of *fragmentation,* as you became torn between people and toys, career and family, leisure and work. Even as you accumulated more possessions, even as you acquired more friends, even as you gathered the trophies of greater achievements, you couldn't quite understand why your heart, and therefore your life, felt increasingly *empty.*

Flower of hope
But still, your heart held the delicate flower of hope. A hope that was fuelled by the mythology of romantic love. A hope that fed your imagination. Somewhere out there was your perfect partner, your soul mate, their moon to your sun, their light bulb to your lampshade, and

the promise of a love so complete, so true, so comforting. You looked, you sought, you searched, ready to collapse the walls and turn on the fountain behind the rusty gates of your heart.

In your desperation, you allowed one or two or maybe three to enter, only to find that their heart was also broken, blocked, frozen, withered, fragmented and empty, in similar ways to your own.

You eventually realized that they too were in a state of neediness and also searching for the sunshine of love to illuminate the lonely darkness of their self isolation. Deep down, you knew two needy people can never satisfy each others 'need' for love. And with each passing encounter, with each disillusion, you suffered a further withering of your own heart, now so parched and dry that hope itself was beginning to fade.

Then one day, one splendidly fateful day, it happened! You caught each other's eyes from across the room and, in one glance, one moment, one magical, stunning moment, you were hooked. This was the mythology of 'love at first sight' come true. 'Falling in love' was real and it was happening to you now. In an instant, your heart surrendered. Walls tumbled, barriers dissolved, the ice melted and out you came, nervously, gratefully, into the light of another's love, somehow trusting, somehow knowing, somehow feeling safe, secure and, most of all, sure... this is it! They are it! Everything else in life became a secondary distraction and you only had thoughts about them. From your first waking moment to the closing thoughts at the end of each day, so strong were the feelings for each other going in both directions, it was as if you were glued together in each other's presence, even when you were hundreds of miles apart.

It would be some time before you would realize that your heart had been *stolen* by them and that you were attempting to steal theirs too.

Just as some children will steal the toys of others under the illusion that they are more deserving, and that the acquisition of the others' toys will make them happy, you try to do the same with another's heart. If only you could have exclusive access, if only you could be the only one to be loved by them, then it would be as if you had won the lottery of the ultimate affection.

Novelty wears off

So the emptiness disappeared, the withering ended, the fragmentation seemed to be healed and the ice melted. But only in their presence, and not for long. Honeymoons end, almost as surely as flowers must wilt. Familiarity soon sets in and you fall back into old patterns. You forget the newness of each other; you tire of the creative discovery of aspects of your self that no-one else has been able to show you in the mirror that is relationship. The novelty wears off, just as it always did with your toys. The honeymoon time, which contained giving, sharing, understanding and much laughter, subsides into routine.

The demise of the relationship is foretold when the first expectation is born. You did not realize that, in your giving and sharing, you were really 'taking' in disguise. You didn't realize the water of another's affection cannot flow constantly in the way you want. You didn't see the real reason why they showed up in your life - to give you a chance to burst your own dam, to give your heart an opportunity to flow out freely as it once did in those innocent times before toys.

In those times, in your innocence, you loved unconditionally, without exclusivity, without fixating on one object or one person. You loved without expectation. Your heart was the fountain of your life and the pathway to connect you with all other life. In those sweet, innocent days, your love was pure. Your love made no judgments, needed nothing, and recognised everyone and everything was equally deserving of your attention and, as you attended, you loved.

The 7 Myths About Love...Actually!

Did you recognize the story? It is a story we all share. Perhaps not in that precise sequence. We all fall prey to a process of assimilating a number of illusions about love and happiness. It is a process that leaves most of us with a heart that feels like it is broken, blocked, frozen, withered, empty, fragmented, stolen. It is a story about how your heart (your consciousness) is gradually *poisoned* by a set of false beliefs, a series of myths about love, which lead us far away from love itself.

These myths are both our inheritance and, if we are not careful, will also be our legacy. Here are the main myths that have evolved and expanded within our consciousness, and to a large extent now our world, without us being aware that they do so.

Myth One:

"Love is Required"

No it's not

We often hear it said, "We all need love, we all need to 'be loved', and know that we are loved." But you don't. If there is a 'need', it is to give love, which simply means to give of oneself, because love is what we are. But you don't know you are love until you open, see and give of your 'self' (not your body!) to something or someone, free of the slightest desire for anything in return. Often referred to as unconditional love.

Give what? It doesn't really matter. It can take the form of time, attention, a gift, some wisdom, guidance, anything. It's not 'what' is given that matters, but the intention. It's not what's visible in the giving, but what is invisible in the offering. We intuitively know that love's intention never seeks anything in return. Loves intention is only to extend, connect and flow. True love is never incomplete, it cannot be added to. It therefore seeks nothing nor needs anything. Love is not an object. It is not something separate from you/I/we. It is you/I/we. Only the language of words make love seem like an object, like something separate.

If love is 'concerned' about anything, then it is concerned with bringing happiness to others. It just takes time to figure out that 'the other' can only be truly happy when they also realize themselves as love, and that only freedom from all neediness is what makes it possible to know and be love. Which means the greatest gift you can give to another is to be love your self, which is the same as saying 'be your self'. This may then spark the other into realizing they too are love, as you show them the way. However, as we shall see, 'being your self' is not quite as easy as it sounds.

At least once a year, you will visit a department store, buy a gift and give that gift to someone in your life saying, "This is from me to you with love". In that moment, you acknowledge where love always lives. Not in the department store (we wish!), not in the gift, not even in the wrapping or the card, but in the giving that originates within you. Which then begs the obvious question, why do we spend our lives searching outside our self for what we already have within our self? A question to which we will later return.

The only way to 'know' love is to give love, which is exactly the same as saying the only way to 'know' your self is to give of your self. And when you do, it becomes obvious that love is not 'required' simply because both the 'self' and 'love' are one and the same. And neither ever runs out! However, 'giving' is not an idea that needs to be thought about. If we have to think about 'giving with love' then it's unlikely to be authentic. But it's better than not giving.

We often 'give' only because we are expected to or we have been taught that we 'should'. We tend to give out of custom or tradition, or sometimes simply out of habit. This is not love, only ritual. Sometimes we give with a smile and an embrace, but if there is the slightest desire to be recognised, or for reciprocation, it's not giving, it's still wanting, still taking. The illusion still persists that love is required. Behind this illusion sits an even more powerful myth, that love can be 'acquired'.

Always Giving is so Tiring!

Some people believe they are always giving, giving, giving, and that it just feels draining and tiring. This only means 'real love' is not yet at work. While the heart is straining to be loving the head is thinking, "You are always taking from me, why don't you give anything back, why don't you just recognise my lovingness." If there is the slightest desire for anything in return, it is not giving but taking. Behind the apparent expression of generosity there is a 'desire' to acquire. And love has no desires for itself. It is the intention to 'get' something, which sits behind the gesture of giving, that generates the negative thinking when there is no reciprocation. And that is the real cause of feeling drained and tired. One sure sign that the energy of love is flowing for real is that it will never be tiring, only energising and empowering.

Myth Two

"Love is Acquired"

Unfortunately it isn't!

The only real energy in life that cannot be acquired is the energy of love. Why? Because you are that energy. You cannot acquire your own self. You cannot acquire your own heart. You cannot acquire what you already are.

Love is not an external energy that you can 'get' and 'keep' and 'store' and 'use' on a rainy day. This truth escapes most people in their search for love. It ensures any search will always fail. The association of romance and love only serves to strengthen this myth, as it teaches us that love in life is only possible when you find the right person for you. The illusion, that when found they will be the 'true source' of love in your life, will keep you looking in the wrong direction i.e. outside and away from your self.

In many schools of psychology and psychiatry, there is a belief that children need to acquire love from their parents. But they don't. They can't. It's an illusion to think that you can 'get your love' from your mother and father. You can receive it but it's not where you get it! The parents true role is not to give love to the child but to 'be love' for the child. Being love is prior to giving love. Being love IS giving love. 'Being love' in every situation and in every relationship teaches, by example, the child how to be love and give of themselves in a clean, pure and unselfish way. Unfortunately most children don't learn this because the parents themselves have learned and then teach, by example, the opposite – that love is 'required' and that it has to be 'acquired' from someone else. Which of course is why so few of us ever realise love is what we are.

In teaching the child that they need a parent's love we teach dependency, one of the foundations of lifelong suffering. In showing the child how to be love, which is how to be themselves, we build the foundation of freedom.

Even more fatally and fatefully, parents also tend to pass on the inherited belief that if you don't acquire the love of others you must not give the love of your self, which is the self. Which is the equivalent of a death sentence for the very spirit we are. Not death in the literal sense, where an ending is created, but the death of the ability to do what we are designed to do, which is to give, radiate, share, extend, connect...selflessly.

To believe that you should not give love until you acquire love is to attempt to kill love, which is spiritual suicide born out of ignorance about love. That's not to say parents should not be loving towards their children a little . if not a lot more than others. But it doesn't help when the parent mistakes 'attachment' for love. This one mistake, when passed on to us as children, will not only be the beginning of our own personal 'true toy story', but if assimilated, it will also diminish our capacity to love (to be our 'self') for the rest of our life. Until you see the difference between attachment and love, happiness will be impossible. Until you are able to detach, love will be impossible. It's not an easy separation, in a world where 'love' and 'attachment' have been married for a long time.

Being and Doing

Although love is primarily a state of being, a pure intention, love also does, love acts. But only when the source of love, the being (the self) knows itself as 'a being' and not 'a doing'! Right now, most of us learn to build our identity around something we do, on specific actions, on a position, on a title. The most common places where we identify with a position or a title is in an organisation or a family (parent/child or senior/junior). And, as long as we identify with what we do, we cannot know, be or give love. We are always seeing ourselves as superior or inferior and love is neither. Love neither looks 'down at' others, or 'up to' others. Which is why, those who create a superior mindset, or an inferior mindset can be uncomfortable in the presence of love.

Myth Three

"You Fall in Love"

Not a Chance!

This is a tough one to 'see' as this myth has permeated almost all forms of romance for centuries. But the truth is you cannot ever 'fall' in love. True love is never a fall; it can never be a descent. Infatuation, obsession and attachment are usually what happen in reality, and then given the term 'falling in love'.

Some of the proofs of love's presence in a relationship include an absence of infatuation, obsession and absolutely no attachment. There isn't the feeling of falling, but an 'uplifting'. There is no sense of confinement but a real sense of freedom within the relationship. There is no 'heat' but a coolness and strength that endures through all circumstances and events.

You can never literally 'fall in love' as you are already, and always will be 'in' love, because you are always and already 'in' your self. Love and the authentic self are one and the same. But if you are not aware of this, and most of us aren't, it can feel like you are falling back into your self, your true self. But it's not a falling, more an awakening to a true awareness of your self. Sometimes it's called self-realization.

Three things can happen when you 'believe' you have fallen in love with another. Not necessarily in this order.

The first happens entirely within your consciousness. You create an idealized image of the other on the screen of your mind and then lose your 'self' in the image. That's why you can't think clearly about anything other than them. That's why you lose your appetite, why you don't really want to talk to anyone else, why your sleeping patterns are affected for days. You become habituated to giving your attention, your self, to the image of the other in your mind.

Losing one's self in the self-created, idealized image of another is not love, it's just attachment, which often becomes infatuation. There is nothing more certain than the illusion coming to an end. This normally happens when the other does something that contradicts your perfect image of them. But even then you will go on idealizing them, even after they fail to live up to your image. This is why you may notice, somewhat curiously at first, that you love some people more when they are not there! But of course it's not real love, it's simply 'idealization'.

The second dimension to the myth of falling in love is the feeling that while you may be miles, sometimes hundreds of miles apart, it is as if you can feel them right next to you. This is an effect that is caused by an exchange of mental energy, a subtle communication between two people, two beings who are radiating energy. Each one is thinking intensely and frequently about the other. Each one is picking up the mental vibrations of the other. Sometimes this can be extremely accurate where specific thoughts of one are crystallized in the mind of the other. Or it can be a strong feeling, a powerful sense of the other's presence. Nothing new here, in the sense that it's possible to transcend the limits of physical communication to higher, subtler levels of communicating and connect with another at that subtler level. Pets are much better at this!

The third dimension to the illusion of 'falling' is known as the 'intimacy of physical presence'. There is a level of comfort in the other's company that allows you to be totally open and vulnerable. That just means you feel you are able to collapse all those walls that you have been erecting around your heart for all those years.

The mutual transparency is such a relief from the pressure of keeping all those walls in place. A pressure you only fully notice when you stop trying to hold the walls up. Now you can share all that is in your heart, in your self, in your consciousness, all your secrets and all the experiences that have been buried away. This is not only a relief but as you share you start to see how small and insignificant those things were, you start to understand your self with a clarity that is not possible until you reveal your self, until you express (press out) your self to another. This absolute openness to the other, reciprocated by the other, co-creates what you will perceive as a special relationship. It is an intimate relationship. A relationship where the idea of intimacy comes fully and energetically alive as each one is implicitly saying to the other, "Come in (in) to (ti) me (ma) and see (cy)" me. And as each allows the other into the other, each enters the energy of the other, which is the same as entering the love of the other, which feels like falling into the love of the other, which in a sense it is, which is then swooningly called 'falling in love'. Only it's not a fall, it's more like a relieving, perhaps a clearing, some resolving, much revealing, so it's probably more accurate to call it therapy! Which is also why it can't and doesn't last. Which is why there is always the 'honeymoon period'. The ending of which is usually signalled by one of three events.

The first signal is when you start to re-erect the walls around your heart when 'they' do something that you either don't like or didn't expect. Or perhaps they push you to go a little too deep into your self, to a place where a wound is still a little too tender, a memory just a little too painful. But of course you won't realize it's you that is the source of your own discomfort, as you are likely to also fall back into the old but fatal belief that they are 'making' you feel this way.

The second 'end of honeymoon' signal is simply the calming of the relationship. And what's left is the ability to be at ease in each other's company at all times in all places. Like finding a shoe that perfectly fits your foot, you have found someone with whom you feel entirely comfortable. This 'fit' then becomes a comfort zone. A zone where not everything is perfect but it's the best so far and why would you want to be with anyone else and go through all that 'revealing' again. Or maybe with someone new you wouldn't go through all that again so you would not have such a powerful 'together story' to cling to and identify with. Some people do stay together simply because of a history that they create together. This story includes the original therapeutic effect, which in itself is remembered as a kind of liberation that seemed to have been granted by the other, but was in truth only facilitated by the other.

The third signal of the end of the honeymoon can be the realisation that love is much bigger than two, that the Kingdom of Love is not called Coupledom. When true love is fully realized it also becomes obvious that it's much bigger than just two people being together. It's much bigger than the limitations of one special relationship, even if that relationship expands into a physical family.

Love is 'the' universal energy and it awaits universal application if it is to be fully known, its full power understood and its beauty seen. This seems to be an innate awareness that we all carry but lose in the routines and struggles of daily living. If this universal sense of loves presence is allowed to bloom the exclusivity of any particular relationship may become too confining and claustrophobic to live within. There may ultimately be a parting of the ways as one or both feel called to be more ...unlimited. Or there may be an attempt to stay in the relationship and still realize the universality of love together. This could be 'challenging' as any attachment is like a denial of that universality, and a new set of walls can easily be created. Or it could be that one recognizes that 'this' is bigger than the two of us, and the other doesn't.

As almost everyone who believes they have fallen in love can verify, honeymoons never last. The 'falling' has to end. There has to be a landing, which often feels like a crash landing! Sometimes that fall is a complete separation and at others there is simply a return to a previous reality with a new insight into the other, "Ah, now I see, now I know, what you are really like." An image is shattered and an illusion destroyed. This is the moment when people either go their separate ways or the shoots of true love emerge in the form of unconditional acceptance of the other, regardless of what they say or do or have said or have already done. But as we shall see it's a hard to maintain that unconditional acceptance when we have spent our life learning expectation, judgement and dependency.

It is the presence of these and other learned habits that give rise to the modern cliché about the intimate relationship that we call marriage when we say, "Ah, but you have to work at a marriage". But perhaps it's not the relationship that requires the work. What takes work is not allowing these habits to interfere with the energy that we bring to any relationship. These habits signify the absence of love and the presence of anger and fear. These inclinations toward judging, criticising and blaming the other indicate there is still an expectation of the other to be a source of love for the self. A common mistake that can eventually turn any relationship into what feels more like a battleground.

 ## An Unconditional Shock

Almost everyone seems to acknowledge that true love is unconditional. Which means almost everyone knows deep down that true love places no condition on caring and sharing, or any form of giving. Love does receive, but it does not take. It may not agree or condone, but it always accepts. It is the basis of our ability to discern what is true from what is false, but it does not judge another. Notice 'where' you 'do' your receiving, accepting and appreciating, and you will see that love arises as your self. And just as you cannot 'see' your self, you will notice you cannot see love, only its expression and its effect. Like electricity love is invisible, but if you touch a bare and live wire with your hand you will feel the shock of an electrical current. Dare to bare your self, to open your self, to remove all that you place between your self and others, dare to give unconditionally of your self, and both you and whoever else is in your presence, are likely to feel the shock of the unconditional energy of life itself, which is love!

Myth Four

"Love is Exclusive"

Unfortunately it isn't

This is the belief that, somewhere out there, there is a 'special one' for me, my 'soul mate', the one who I am fated to be with for the rest of my life. This is truly the stuff of Hollywood movies and the myth of romantic love. We learn to limit the idea of love to one other special person or to some very exclusive relationships, often within our own family. We make love small and appropriate only to those whom we believe and perceive as special people in our life and therefore deserving of our love.

In truth, real love can never be small and exclusive. It is, as we innately sense, inclusive. It does not have preferences, it does not select, it does not think I will love him/her more than him/her. Real love accepts and
. embraces all, without a second thought, without even a first thought. It does not judge, condemn or criticise the other in any way.

There is no one 'soul mate'. When we are being our self i.e. being love itself, we are all 'soul' mates for each other. This is only possible when we have seen through the illusions that love is exclusive and selective. So what about mating? The deepest reason we tend to be a little 'mixed up' about love is due to one simple and recurring mistake. We believe we are the body that we occupy. Identifying with our physical form has the effect of reducing our connection to others to some physical sensation - sight, sound and touch being the three main ways that we connect and communicate with others. This largely, if not entirely, reduces our perception of love to a physical action/exchange.

We reduce everything to the physical and evaluate everything at a physical level including beauty, fun, happiness, joy etc. And that's when our awareness of love, and the ability to be our self and to give of our self, is temporarily lost. All because we lose our awareness of who I AM. When we believe we are physical then we are constantly seeking sensation which means 'taking' something 'in and through' our senses. Sensual stimulation is then confused with love.

This is why there is no such thing as 'making love'. Ironically it is the one thing that can never be made. Love is already made. It is what makes everything else. Although 'making love' is just a figure of speech it has become embedded in our language to such an extent that it's often given the status of a literal truism. It obviously most often refers to 'having sex'. Having sex is not making love, it's having sex. And sex is mostly a physical action very often containing little unconditional giving and more often much conditioned wanting and taking. Hence the 'having' in the having sex. It can be a glorious 'sensation', hence its glorification, but there can be very little love involved and certainly love is not 'made' in the process. Some intimate contact perhaps, the conception of a new babies form most certainly, but not love. Love is the maker not the made.

That is not to say that sex is bad or wrong, just to say it's best not to confuse it with love. Is sex an expression of love? It can be, however the physical sensation is so powerful, so physically 'ecstatic', and therefore it's memory so powerful, it easily becomes another physical craving. Slightly higher in the league table than ice cream, but a craving never the less. Any craving means love is not present, love is not extending and connecting, love is contracting, because the self is contracting just to satisfy a craving. That craving is essentially a form of 'lusting'. And lusting is obviously not loving.

If you dare whisper this insight, even softly, you can expect an emotional reaction in return. When love is mentioned in the same sentence as lust and the truth of each is 'exposed', then what has become one of the most powerful drugs of this modern age is threatened. Whisper this not at all to the monthly glossy magazines whose sales are almost entirely dependent on the mythology that love and sex are synonymous. For if they as much as whisper this within their magazines, then their magazines would be no more. Such is the power of the drug. And it's probably not a good idea to mention it to your partner until they have also 'read the book'!

It can appear to be a huge jump from love as an exclusive relationship to love as a unconditional and benevolent intention. It is a jump that would seem to propel the self into instant sainthood. It's therefore easy to dismiss such a shift as unrealistic in this modern and somewhat sexualised world, and therefore impossible. But as we continue our investigation into the true meaning of love we may discover each of us is not only a source of love in the world, it is the very nature of every human being. Or as 'they' do say, "Inside each one of us there is a saintly being awaiting repatriation to the world". Now who said that? Mmm!

 ## Souls Don't Mate

There is no such thing as a soul mate basically because souls don't mate. Only bodies mate. A soul mate is just a very strong affinity with another. There is likely to be a high level of resonance at the mental level which allows both to communicate at subtle levels beyond words. We all have the capacity to develop this subtler level of communication. The 'wiring' is already there, but we seldom learn how to activate it. So dependent have we become on sounds, words, pictures and the technology that delivers them, we no longer develop and deploy our subtler senses. So agitated and distracted by the world 'out there' have we become, that we take little or no time simply to be quiet. And quietness is the essential inner condition to receive the subtle, radiant energy of another. And when we do it may dawn upon our awareness that we are already connected. It is a connection that can never be broken, only ignored. We are all already mates, or mated, it's just we don't pick up each other's signals unless we are on exactly the same wavelength Occasionally we meet someone who seems capable of making friends with anyone and everyone. They know how to mate at the deepest level, which simply means resonate and connect with 'the other' regardless of who the other is or appears to be on the surface.

Myth Five

"Love is Attachment"

Never, but it's hard to fathom

One of the most common myths that stalks the world today is that love is attachment. What is seldom 'noticed' is that where there is attachment there is fear. Fear of loss or damage to the object of attachment. And fear is not love. Where there is fear there cannot be love. Fear is love distorted by attachment.

Whenever you are attached to anything, an object, person, place or just an idea, your heart is blocked. The energy that emanates naturally from your heart, which means from you, is distorted into different wavelengths or vibrations, as it makes its way past the object of attachment in your mind and out into the world. You are therefore unable to be open and give of your self fully and whole heartedly. You are not able to be consistently loveful or loving. Fear will be present, in the foreground or in the background of your awareness, in one of its various forms such as anxiousness, tension, worry or you are just plain scared.

Just as a coloured filter changes the colour of the light radiating from a spotlight onto the stage, so any attachment is like a filter that distorts the energy, the light of love, that emanates naturally from the self, often blocking that light completely. You know when this is happening when you 'feel' some form of emotion. Emotion is a signal that you are attached to some thing that is 'on your mind'. It is the idea or image of the object of attachment that is 'on your mind' that is blocking your heart, your love, you. Only detachment, or non-attachment, can re-open 'you' and restore your capacity to be loveful and loving.

An obsession with anything or anyone, is sometimes mistaken for love, but it's simply an extreme form of attachment. In the moment that you obsess there is a complete blockage. It's as if you are almost incapable of giving energy to anything or anyone except the object of your obsession. When obsessed with anything you are using the object of attachment, the object of your obsession, to define your self.

Worrying about someone whom you call a 'loved one' isn't love, it isn't caring, it's worrying, so it is fear. The fear arises because you are attached to your loved one. The truth is revealed by the presence of your worry (fear). In the light of that truth you may see they are not your 'loved one', they are your 'attached one'! And, as an increasing number of people are beginning to realise, you cannot be love and therefore give love, if you are attached to anything or anyone.

The belief that love is known and expressed through attachment is one of the most powerful myths that is programmed into human consciousness. It sits at the heart of almost all tradition and culture. It defines lifestyles and shapes destinies. It generates conflict and it creates and sustains all the suffering that we call stress. In Part II we explore the precise mechanism of attachment, why we attach so frequently, how to 'detach' and why detachment is essential to what is sometimes referred to as the healing of the heart. Ask almost anyone who has strolled down any authentically spiritual path and they are likely to concur with the idea that you cannot love unless you are detached. But to the vast majority this is just one big paradox to the modern mind.

Are YOU Watching?

The next time you notice your self reacting negatively to any person or situation take a moment to reflect. Acknowledge that you are the creator of your reaction and not the other person. Sit quietly with the memory of your reaction, just watch it as you slowly replay on the screen of your mind. Don't judge it, don't criticise it, don't try to justify it. Just watch it. You will begin to see behind your reaction to what you are attaching to in your mind, and how that is the cause of your reactivity. Love doesn't react emotionally to anyone or anything. It always responds with acceptance and an ability to embrace the other. It always responds with understanding, compassion and the grace to be with the other. Only attachment reacts.

Myth Six

"Love Hurts"

Not true

The opposite is true. If it hurts, it's not love. There is a classic scene in the restaurant. At the start of the evening the young couple are gazing romantically into each others eyes over dinner. Any observer might think, "Look, isn't that sweet". But as the evening wears on the energy changes and little arguments start to break out, until finally one storms away from the table in anger, with the other in hot pursuit. The observer can then be heard to say, "Aw, look, they're having a quarrel, a 'lovers tiff', they must be so in love". But anger is not love. Anger is anger. Like fear, anger is a sign that love is absent. Anger is emotional pain.

It's true to say that most intimate relationships will have their ups and downs. There will be moments of conflict and personal suffering. But this has nothing to do with love and more to do with judgement and blame, expectation and attachment, dependency and jealousy. In those moments love is not present, it is temporarily lost. Love doesn't create conflict, it doesn't suffer, it doesn't argue, it has nothing to do with any kind of pain. Love cannot create hurt, it is the healer of hurt. Hurt is always a product of the ego. Where there is ego, love is not. Ego is the darkness that imprisons the light of love. It is what we all learn to do. It is why freedom from stress so often seems impossible. Even the holiest of the holy saints and sages are likely to have the darkness of the ego suppressing their light. They are simply more aware of it, wiser about it, and therefore more able to deal with it, than the rest of us.

Most hurt arises from one simple but prevalent illusion that others are responsible for our feelings. This is the belief that runs the world today and says, "It's not me, it's them!" The truth is much closer to the reverse. We are each totally responsible for our feelings, for the emotions that we create and feel, at all times in all situations. It's not difficult to prove.

Reflect on a past relationship when someone said something negative to you and about you, and it didn't bother you for one moment. But then they said something similar on another day, but this time you felt terrible and reacted accordingly (emotionally). It's always *you* that makes you feel whatever you feel at each and every moment...always. This truth is not easy to see and to put into practice. It's not easy to live, because just about every waking moment of life so far has been about learning and living the 'other' way, living from the belief that 'it's them, not me'!

This is why judgment, blame and expectation loom large in our head as we relate to and interact with others. This is why love disappears from the reality of our daily life so regularly and, on some days doesn't show up at all. Only the realization of complete 'self-responsibility' can begin to end our entirely self inflicted 'hurts', and restore our capacity to be loving.

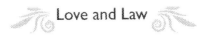

Love and Law

Finding that balance between love and law, the iron fist in the velvet glove, is perhaps the greatest challenge for anyone who is learning to play the role that comes with a position. There is a tendency to associate love with niceness and sweetness. And of course love is a nice energy to give and to receive in whatever form. There is a sweetness in the nature of one who is loving. But too much sweetness and things can start to get 'sticky'. Sticky means attachment is present. Neediness will be sensed in the one who is obviously too sweet, too often, and more often during moments when other expressions of love are more appropriate. Tough love is not a new idea but a hard one to practice when you feel needy within your self. While tough love is necessary in any parent/child, teacher/student or manager/employee relationship, if the parent/teacher/manager are needy in themselves, they will not be able to lay down the law, as is their role, with love. Law without love is simply a dictatorship, inviting only alienation. But love without law invites chaos. Many managers/teachers/parents sabotage their own effectiveness when they themselves are needy of approval and acceptance from others. Only when those dependencies have been healed can they lovingly and lawfully connect with others and win the co-operation of others to lovingly comply with the law.

Myth Seven

"Love is Lost"

Not possible

Love is what you are and you can never lose your self. So what are you exactly if you are love? This is not an easy description to grasp as it takes us into the intangible territory of the self, of the 'I' that says 'I am'. To visit this territory and both realise and 'feel' the reality of love, we begin with a visualisation, segway into contemplation and end with a meditation.

Imagine a diamond made only of radiant light. It is totally transparent. Anything or anyone can enter the diamond of lights radiance and, as they do, they are embraced by that light, touched and enlightened by that light. You can see into and through the light, so nothing within it is hidden. That light radiates in all directions and whatever or whoever that light touches, feels nourished and uplifted.

As the radiant light of the diamond (that is made of radiant light) touches everything, it's as if it also contains everything. It has no intention of being other than what it is, no motive to acquire anything from whoever or whatever it embraces. It is as if that light knows that it is already all that it can be. This is the light of love, the light of the self. You are that light. Each of us is such a light.

Take a moment to see in your minds eye these images of radiance. Contemplate the idea that the energy of you, is like such a light. Not a light that is seen by physical eyes. Not a light that is reflected by a mirror. Simply a radiant energy emanating from the conscious being that you are. As you contemplate this idea sense how the first 'thing' that you touch and embrace with your light is the body that you occupy. Sense how your light fills the room that you currently occupy. How it touches the people around you in that room. Then imagine that light, your light, reaching beyond the room to touch and embrace all those in your life that you know. And then reaching beyond 'the known' as it radiates out into the world, touching, enfolding and connecting with who knows what or who! You don't need to know. It's not important.

Now take a moment and meditate on this awareness described by those words and see if you can begin to 'feel' the reality of them for your self. As you do you will come to realise the light of you 'is' the light of love. It's not a fairy story, its not some romantic tale about fairy 'lights'. It is what you are. It is what you do. It is the way of love. It is the way of being.

So it's not possible to lose love because you cannot lose your self. You cannot lose the light that you are, or the capacity to radiate that subtle, invisible, intangible radiant energy that you are.

The illusion, that 'love is lost', simply occurs when you forget your self and believe you are some thing other than your self. This tends to happen every time you do look in the mirror and mistake your self for what you see in the mirror! It's that moment when you frighten your self awake in the morning! But you are not a face! When you make your face lovely, you don't make your self lovely. So even if you have a pretty face, 'you' are not a pretty face. You are not a material body, so when you make your body look lovely you don't make your self look lovely. You wear a face and you inhabit a body, but true loveliness cannot be reflected in a mirror. True loveliness is invisible to the naked eye.

If you think pretty faces and bodies denote loveliness or love, it is an illusion that makes you forget your self and seek love. This is a delusion that is visited upon us every day by the face and body industries. And as your body loses its shape and it's 'looks', as it must, you start to believe you will lose love. It is our acceptance of these illusions, our continued absorption of these delusions, that perfectly sustains our confusions about love.

So let's back up and reflect a little more on what is apparently one of the most frequently asked question on Google which is 'What is LOVE ...exactly?'

If you knew love as 'I am'

If you knew your self as love

You would never want anything ever again

You would never attempt to take anything from anyone ever again

You would realize YOU don't ever 'need' anything – only your body has needs but YOU don't

You would become naturally detached from and yet intimately connected to everything and everyone

There would no longer be any dependency on anything or anyone

No-one could ever hurt you and you could never intend to hurt another

You would know that you could never lose anything 'real' ... ever again

You would be able to respond to the suffering of others without suffering yourself

You would know exactly what makes other people so unhappy

And you would know the secrets of being happy in your self

If only you knew

But you do know

Don't you remember?

What on Earth is LOVE?

The universal symbol of love is the heart. When the heart is known, love is known. The terms *soul, spirit, heart, self* are almost synonymous, all referring to our authentic spiritual self, which is both conscious and aware. The heart is not some thing separate from what the 'I' that says 'I am' is. However this level of self awareness is not something that we learn. We are more often 'body aware', or aware of the presence of some stressful emotions, or aware of what's happening in the world 'out there'. Explore what follows and see if it 'rings true' for you in the light of your own **ex**perience and **in**sperience.

A Glimpse of Two Hearts

We each have two hearts. One is frequently confused with the other. The first heart is the one in your body. It's the strongest pump in the world, designed to operate 24/7 and move massive quantities of oxygenated blood through the physical systems of your body. Normally it operates at around 60 to 90 beats per minute but, if you start to create fearful thoughts in your mind, it will increase to around 120 beats per minute. Which brings us to your other heart or the heart of YOU, which is ...YOU!

The second heart is the heart of your consciousness. Entirely non-physical and therefore non-material. It is your spiritual heart, sometimes referred to as the soul or the authentic self.

It's not something separate from you, not another organ in your body, it is (you are) the animating energy of your body. It is (you are) invisible to the physical eye; it is (you are) the 'inner space' of consciousness, where you are just being…your self.

Everyone has (is) a good heart, because the original nature of every heart, of every human being, is goodness. This goodness can never be lost only hidden (suppressed) from awareness. Like the physical heart, if your spiritual heart, which is you, is polluted by anything toxic such as some of the beliefs/myths about love that we explored earlier, or by memories of hurt, or by the habits of fear or anger, this 'pollution' of the atmosphere of your consciousness will cloud that original goodness and adversely affect the wellness of your being.

Consequently, the quality of energy that you then give to the form that you animate (your body), to your immediate relationships and to the wider world, will be toxic, or what is sometimes called negative.

If your physical heart is overworked and unrested, over a period of time it will weaken and break down. Whereas if the heart of your consciousness, your spiritual heart, you, is under used and under exercised, it will feel like it is atrophying, decaying and therefore losing strength. A distinct absence of joy, enthusiasm and optimism, and the presence of apathy, sorrow and hopelessness will be the main symptoms of the atrophy of your spiritual heart.

Within you, the conscious self, is your mind. Your mind is not an organ of the body, but a 'faculty' of your consciousness. It is where you create your thoughts and 'do' your thinking. Too much mental stimulation, either from outside (e.g. movies) or from inside (e.g. memories), and the mind (thoughts) will race, creating chaos within the energy of your consciousness and disturbing both your spiritual heart (you) and the heart of your body (psychosomatic effect) and your pulse may accelerate.

While the heart of your body is designed to move blood and oxygen to all corners of the body, the heart of your consciousness, your spiritual heart, you, is designed to move the light of love, the unpolluted, subtle energy of consciousness, of you, out into the world of your relationships, through your thoughts, feelings and actions.

The Breath of the Heart

What happens in the physical dimensions of time and space is often the opposite of what happens in the spiritual dimension i.e. consciousness, which is beyond time and space. Our physical body needs to consume air, water and food to gain energy, grow, build strength and stay healthy. But as spiritual beings we need to share our energy, our light, our love, in order to build spiritual strength and empower (energise) our self. We know this when we feel the satisfaction of giving is much greater than taking or even receiving. We know this in the lightness we 'feel' during and following any benevolent act. Your body 'needs' to consume food to stay strong, whereas your spirit, you, need (if it can be called a need) to give of your self to stay strong, to remain powerful, within your self.

Another way to look at it is this. What is the key element that constitutes much of the material of the physical world including our body? And what is the one ingredient that unites us all at the physical level? It is oxygen. It is the common constituent of air and water. The atmosphere of the world is filled with oxygen. Without air, your body would die an almost instant death. Without water, it would die a gradual death. Both contain the vital ingredient we call oxygen. The oxygen within air and water keep your body alive.

But the spiritual heart of a human being is not in need of oxygen. The vital force, the revitalizing energy that we each need, is love. Not as something that has to be to acquired, but as the invisible energy that is designed to be 'expired'. Not expired as in 'ended', but expired as in radiated outwards. 'Oxygen in' and the body's health is enriched and sustained. 'Love out' and the soul/self is enriched and sustained. So you could say 'love is … the oxygen of the soul'. It is the pure essence of the being that I/you/we are. It is the highest vibration of the self, of the 'I' that says 'I am'. It is the light of consciousness. It is the light of every being. It is the light that never goes out. A light that radiates in all directions through all dimensions. But obviously not a light that you will ever see with physical eyes.

In many ways we could view life as one long parallel breathing exercise! Just as our bodies need to consume food and give out waste, breathe in oxygen and breathe out CO_2, so 'the self' needs to breathe in and breathe out (receive and give) the energy of love. While both the 'out' and 'in' breaths are vital for both hearts, it could be said that, for the body, the most important is the 'in breath', but for the spiritual heart, for you, the most important is the 'out breath', ie. the giving of our self without condition or desire for any return, often referred to as selflessness.

The Light of the Heart

We all seem to intuitively know that true loves intention and expression is unconditional. When the light of our love (self) receives the light of another (love), it's not a need that is being satisfied, it's just a re-union, a re-integration of two lights. Switch on any two lights in the same room and, while you can see the individual sources of light you cannot see where the radiance of one intersects with the other; the whole room just becomes brighter. Each light does not need the other, but the whole room is grateful for the light of all…if rooms were grateful… so to speak!

If we do have a need, it is for the light of another's love to show us how to illuminate our endarkened consciousness until we learn to shine our own light again. Sometimes someone appears in our life who plays that role. Someone whose love is like a bright light. But we often mistake their role in our life as someone requiring our devotion and even worship when, in reality, they are only present to show us how to switch on our own light and dispel our own darkness. And if they do encourage our dependency upon them it just means they have lost their way, their light is also blocked, and they need us to need them. True love is always free of any form of dependency or co-dependency at the spiritual level, otherwise it wouldn't be love.

The Movement of the Heart

In the simplest of terms, love is a vibration of the energy of the self. It is not easy to perceive and give true love if we have spent our life, as most have, believing we are only physical forms and therefore only having one heart, the one behind our rib cage. Yet most of us know that true, 'heartfelt' love is not a tangible experience. It is an intention that 'moves' the giving of a gift, the caring for another, the compassion towards others.

Just as the breeze invisibly moves the leaves on the tree, love invisibly discerns, intends, shapes itself to meet the needs of another. Love is that light that radiates through the eyes in a glance. As it travels through the eyes of the other it touches their heart, it touches their 'self'. Though it cannot be seen by the eyes through which it radiates, it is felt and known by both the 'radiator' and by the receiver.

True Love

There is no such thing as 'true' love, in the sense that there is no such thing as untrue love. Love is simply mistaken for something that it is not, just as we mistake our self for something that we are not. When you understand that you can never go away from what and where you are, you will see that love is never lost, simply obscured, avoided, ignored or suppressed. But, like you, love is always present. Always there with you because it is you, even when you have forgotten that you are you! If that all sounds a little vague or cryptic, it's because words, ideas and concepts are inadequate to capture the very 'energy' that is beyond definition and conceptualization.

Just as the light of one candle can illuminate a darkened room, true love is like a thousand candles that can dispel the darkness of fear and hate in the 'room' of human consciousness. And as it does, it will have a powerful effect on the consciousness of others.

Not yet captured in a test tube, not yet subject to industrial manufacture, not yet packaged for a window display, we all know love as the unseen, intangible energy that quenches the thirst of the one who has forgotten how to be love themselves. We all know love as the healer of division, the preventer of stress and the dissolver of conflict. We all know love as the invisible glue of all harmonious relationships.

The Feelings of the Heart

So what exactly happens in a true exchange of love? What is love's true nature? We are all surrounded everywhere at every moment by various forms of light including X-rays, microwaves, ultraviolet waves and cosmic waves. Many pass straight through our bodies. We cannot see them because they are of a different spectrum/wavelength/vibration than physical light. Love is a vibration of our spiritual light, of the light of our consciousness. Totally invisible to physical eyes yet we feel it, as we radiate it, and we feel it as we receive the radiation of another.

The 'feeling of love' is therefore a perception of a connection between self and other. It is a felt union of two spiritual hearts that are touching through an exchange of their energies in a vibration called love. When the light of the early morning sun touches the flower, it opens to reveal its beautiful form and it releases a sweet fragrance in return. So too, when we are 'touched' by the true love of another we open out and give back the fragrance of our appreciation in return. Love reciprocates love.

In a human relationship this invisible, but felt, connection does not diminish our sense of individuality, but it does dissolve any barriers placed between two souls, between two hearts. Those barriers tend to be made of beliefs and thoughts about the other. These barriers are divisions that are erected by the self and held in the mind, and this is what denies the energy of our love its radiant exit into the world and into our connections with others. It is also these mental barriers, these judgments and beliefs about the other, that block the light of the other's radiant vibration from entering into the inner world of our consciousness, our self. Hence the saying, "True love makes no judgments".

When this link between two spiritual hearts is restored, it frees the soul/self from attachment and dependency on the other. As we saw earlier, contrary to many of our modern mythologies, including those of our friends in Hollywood, love is not attachment and it is not dependent. But once the link of love is broken, once the connection appears to be broken, what is left is the memory of the beauty of that link, and it is the memory that can generate the craving and searching for the real thing again. You can only search for something that you have lost, something that was once present.

In the externalized search to satisfy the craving for that memorised insperience of beauty, attachment is born, neediness sets in and dependency easily becomes the new 'condition' of the heart. (self/soul). And that is then mistaken for love.

So why so much confusion about love, why so much attachment to the 'one I love' or the 'things I love', why do we use the word love so much but feel true love so little? (forgive my generalisation). Could the simplest reason be that we have forgotten that our true heart is not our physical heart, it is our spiritual heart? Which is the same as saying we have forgotten who/ what we are, soul not body, consciousness not matter, spirit not form.

Holding onto the belief, that we are only physical, causes the belief that love is only physical, something to be searched for, found, taken, acquired, stored and consumed at a physical level. Hence we look for love in the wrong way in the wrong place. And that may just explain why there are now so many people wondering why we seem to be living in an increasingly loveless world.

In order to clearly see and understand why we lose awareness of our selves as love, of ourselves as spiritual beings, of each other as radiant sources of love, it's time for another story. It is a story that features your self and your oldest, closest and dearest companion in this world. It is a companion who doesn't want you to find true love which really means finding and knowing your authentic self. Because if you do, he will have to die!

Why You Cannot Love Your Self!

Love is a name for the pure awareness and radiance of consciousness when it is free of all attachment, free of all attempts to possess, hold on, own or acquire. It is what you are. To say "I love my self", is only to sustain an illusion that there is an 'I' and a 'self', when in truth there is only the 'I' that says 'I am'. The I is the self. So you cannot love your self. Love cannot love love. Neither the self nor love is an object. Love just is because you just are. End of story.

Part TWO

A
TRUE
Story

Also your story.
But remember, it's just a story.

Are you sitting comfortably?

Once upon a time...

When you first arrived, at a moment you would come to call your birth, you didn't know who or what you were. You were not even aware that you were in a body. You weren't anybody, you were not a body, you were a no body. In a baby's body, you were unaware that you were a baby, as you had no awareness of separation.

As you looked out through two eyes you were not even aware that you had eyes. You were mesmerised by a multi-coloured, multi-formed, multi-sensory world that, as far you were concerned (although you were not concerned about anything), was NOT outside you, because you had not yet learned there was an outside. All there was, was what was appearing. The joy and delight at this dance of light put a sparkle in your eyes, a big smile on your face and lots of goo goo gaa gaa gurgling noises started to emerge from the mouth you had not yet realized you had.

The first big surprise came when someone put an object in front of what you would soon learn was your body's hand. And as you touched, you felt the sensation of touch and the shock of perceiving, for the first time, some thing that seemed to be separate from you. Up until that point you were under the impression everything that was appearing was you. You didn't think that, because you had not yet learned to think, it was just so, within the innocence of your awareness.

Slowly but surely the faces of those big people, whom you would later come to know as parents, began to show up with great regularity and do much smiling and laughing. More interestingly, whenever one of these facial images appeared in your awareness, there was a warm feeling, as if a light was shining into your being. But even then you had no sense of a light coming from outside you, because you yourself were just radiating your own light.

Sometimes, when one of these faces did not smile, you felt the beginnings of a dull ache within yourself, and the impulse to frown would make the journey from your heart to appear on your face. In those moments, long since consigned to your deep subconscious memory, you were reflecting the light, the vibration, of the other in the mirror of your own light.

Over the next few days and weeks (of which you were totally unaware) ,those faces would talk and touch and laugh and look at you in such a way that you slowly became aware of separateness. Gradually the power of the physical sensations coming to you through your body would hammer home a new reality, i.e. that you had a form, a body, that was coming under your control. Suddenly you could touch and hold things that previously were just images floating through your awareness. Eye to hand, sight to touch, co-ordination began to grow and you realized that what had previously appeared to be you was really out there, separate from you. Your face would frequently reflect this growing confusion and a creased forehead would tell the story of occasional moments of confusion as you learned to navigate the solid world.

In the meantime, those big people were coming and going and you became more and more aware that you were being picked up and put down, touching and not touching, being laughed at and not being laughed at. Being totally and completely open, you were sensitive to their moods, so that if their emotions were up or down you were affected. Without knowing exactly what you were feeling, you could feel their feelings, even when they were not present in the same room. But you were only dimly aware of the connection between what you were feeling and them.

As your sense of separation increased, and as those big people showed you objects and made sounds, you started to do the same. You began to realize you would be rewarded by a big surge of nice warm feelings from them when you learned to make noises that you would later come to know as words, then phrases, then ideas and then concepts. However, the language that you learned was also the language of separation, and slowly you began to realize your isolation, you were on your own, you were... different. You learned that, in their perception, you were a little boy or girl, that you were a beautiful boy or girl, that you had lovely face, or that you had a small head or you had a naughty personality, that you were good or you were bad.

You innocently believed what they said about you. Your self image and sense of identity began to take shape. But you didn't know that what you were learning, what you were being taught, about your self, was non-sense and therefore nonsense. You had no idea that you were being programmed by the prevailing myths and beliefs of the world around you. And that the primary programme was called 'My Various Identities'.

Before you knew it, you were part of a family and if the name of the family was Smith, then you were the latest little Smith. You kept hearing the word David or Mary and so you became a David or a Mary. When you went to your first school you assimilated the identity of that school. As you played with friends, you imitated heroes and 'stars' from TV, as you learned to identify your self with them. When you got your first passport, you assimilated your national identity. When you achieved some qualifications, a new professional identity was added to the list. Your first job brought two new identities based around what you did and the position that you held. You got married and started to have 'my children' and you went home to 'my family' so you created a family identity.

Eventually you would carry around multiple identities. And when any one of those identities was threatened in any way, if only by your own imagination, you would feel anxious and insecure. In time this anxiety would turn into moments of anger as you learned to use anger to defend one or many of your various identities. You occasionally wondered why life was increasingly punctuated with darker moments. Moments you would later identify as stress. And while there were many good times of 'apparent' happiness and joy, they were also becoming increasingly shorter and shallower as life seemed to accelerate around you. As time passed at what sometimes seemed like a frightening pace it started to feel as if you had to do more faster to maintain your grip on all your various identities.

Amidst this increasing busyness, where a combination of working to survive alongside managing multiple identities takes almost all your time and attention, it would be hard to see that your stress, your emotional suffering, and your unhappiness was always self-created. The prevailing myths that you absorbed and assimilated over so many years since childhood kept you convinced that, "It's not me, it's them", that are making you feel like this. This learned belief would sustain one of your most frequent false identities which says, "I am the victim". As you identified your self as victim, you increasingly interpret events and circumstance so as to affirm your victimhood.

As the levels of stress and discomfort began to rise there was an growing sense that there must be more to life than 'this', more to life than living defensively or offensively, more to life than living just to survive. You began to consciously search for reasons and solutions to your unhappiness, to your grumpiness, to your stressfulness and your sorrows. During your search you started to see that you have spent your life believing you are something or someone that you are not. You had been pretending! You began to notice how the accumulation and assimilation of a whole variety of identities was the underlying cause of your frustrations and your fears, your stress and therefore your unhappiness. Not only were you pretending to be something/someone that you are not, everyone else was and is doing it too, but without being aware they are pretending. You even realised that you were pretending not to know that you were pretending!

Slowly but surely you begin to delete the 'My Various Identities' programme from operating system known as consciousness, as you endeavour to bring an ending to pretending.

The Ending of Pretending

The First Pretend

"I am my Body"

Not true!

If you scan just about any ancient spiritual text, research almost any of the world's spiritual gurus and if you listen to almost all the modern day teachers of enlightenment, they almost all concur on one thing, perhaps the only thing – you are not the form that you occupy. You are not what is reflected back to you when you look in the bathroom mirror in the morning. But as we saw in our story, it's almost the first thing that you are taught to believe that you are. It's the first pretend in a long list of pretences! And when you believe you are that object staring back at you from the mirror, then a hundred other beliefs come rushing to grab you by the spiritual throat and make your life a misery. It's a kind of misery that we all learn to live with.

One belief in particular sits in the background of your consciousness throughout your life and that's the belief in your mortality, that you will die, because that is what bodies do. When you pretend to be your body you also start to pretend that your life will come to an end. From this one belief in endings, all fear is created. All fear comes from the belief that some thing or some one, most especially the self, will end. This includes the belief in the loss of something or someone, which is really the end of possessing something or someone. Fear is stress. Fear is suffering. But we learn to disguise it or justify it as we pretend to accept it as natural and necessary. Little do we realise that where there is fear there cannot be love.

There is of course absolutely no way to scientifically prove that you, the 'I' that says 'I am', is quite a different entity from the body that you occupy, animate and use. But it's at least worth taking note of many well-recorded anecdotal experiences of OBEs (Out of Body Experiences) and NDE's (Near Death Experiences). Notice also how granny's body is becoming more wrinkled by the day, but granny, or granddad for that matter, are just as likely to be going into their second childhood as their spirit becomes lighter and more childlike the older their body becomes. So what's getting older and what's not? Take note of the very verifiable experience of your body being 'located' the room it is in at this moment. It cannot be anywhere else. But 'you' can leave the room right now and go off into another dimension and totally lose awareness of your body and the room. Who did that? What did that? What was it that left the immediate three dimensions of the room and entered a fourth dimension. You did. The self. The 'I' that says 'I am'. The being that has no name but pretends to have a name!

What is more real, your finger or your thought about your finger? What's closer to you, the finger or the thought of the finger? You can get the finger into a test tube for all to see but you cannot get your thought into a test tube. Who creates the thought? You do! So you are the creator of something you cannot cut, burn, drown, touch or taste! Something that is non physical. What does that imply about you the creator? The same! Also something non-physical.

These thoughts and insights into the authentic self are not new. But you can never hear them enough. The world around you is set up in such a way as to both encourage and help you to keep pretending to be a body! It's in 'their' interest to keep you in 'pretend mode' as they rely on you to pay them to help you to sustain the pretence!

You may now know, in theory, who and what you really are, but as soon as you put down this book, start worrying about work, putting on your make-up, complaining about the weather, criticizing someone else, hoping for a better life tomorrow, it means the penny has not yet dropped. You are still seeing and living in the world through a mistaken sense of identity. Therefore the most common form of fear, which is anxiety, will almost certainly be a constant presence in the background of your daily life.

Translating the theory about the 'authentic self' into the actual realization of the true you, takes a little time and some patience. Much depends on how regularly introspective you are, how much you appreciate solitude, how prepared you are to experiment with being 'in silence,' the time you give to some meditative practice and the value you place upon quiet contemplation. All of these inner movements within your consciousness contribute to the reawakening of your true self awareness and the integration of that awareness into you day-to day activities. They all contribute the end of the first and deepest pretend.

How Many Times?

The 'not new' idea of being a non-material entity also raises the 'not new' concept of many lifetimes in many different forms, what some call reincarnation or rebirth. On the one hand, rebirth can answer/explain many different and difficult questions about life, the universe and almost everything. But on the other hand, it's a bit of a distraction. And like the existence of the self or soul, it can never be scientifically proved. At this stage it doesn't really matter, although an understanding of your journey through many lifetimes can help to explain many things, like why you are born into certain circumstances, and why you seem to be born with certain character traits, and why you were fated to have certain 'others' around you, it's just an intellectual, speculative distraction until you realise and understand your self in the here and now. Only when you really see and know your self more intimately, only when you see and understand how you work in conscious and unconscious ways, only when you sense your own infinity, your own eternity, as a self-aware being, only then will such questions be relevant and the answers be of real value.

The Second Pretend

"I am a Boy/Girl"

Actually... neither!

The first 'pretend', that you are a body, is the basis of all the other 'pretendings' that you learn. Which means you are not your gender. That belongs to the body but not to the 'self'. We are all both male and female in the sense that we all contain the potential to develop both male and female traits and tendencies of character or personality. But we are conditioned early in life to 'identify' with one and not the other, and therefore to pretend to be one or the other.

When we demonstrate what we are taught to believe are the right traits for our gender, we receive the encouragement, recognition and affirmation of others that we are being a good female or male, that we are on the right track. Others' approval becomes our reward and eventually it becomes a dependency. This further encourages us to develop some (female/male) character traits and to suppress others. Yes, there are hormonal influences. But hormones are of a physical nature and, with the practice of concentration and meditation, you can (and many do) learn not to be mentally influenced by the effect of your body's chemicals upon our mind.

We all know someone in a female form who is more masculine than many males, and vice versa. Which is about as close as you will get to proof, if proof were required, that your true identity is gender free. Unfortunately that's not the way of the world of products and lifestyles, the world of magazines and sports, or the world of clubs and spas. All of which have a vested interest in you keeping up your pretence.

In almost all spheres of life gender is emphasized as a vital part of our identity. Hence men going to war over woman and woman going to war over men, where war means any level of conflict. All because we mistakenly believe we are our gender. But gender is just the most basic 'body type'.

In your essence you are not a body type. Are you a body type? You occupy a body type, but it's not what you are, just as you can occupy your house but the house is not you.

When the gender belief, the gender illusion, is seen through, when it is seen for what it is, which is just part of the early programming, you free your self of certain misery making habits. Habits like comparing your body with other's, is always a great way to sabotage your self-esteem. Habits like worrying about what others may think about how you look, always a great way to practise for the world worry championships. Habits like fretting over what to wear, what to buy - always guaranteed to empty your pockets. Habits like face painting, muscle pumping, hormone supplementing, all brilliant ways to sustain your insecurity. Habits like attempting to defy the aging process, and perhaps even seeking the elixir of eternal youth, both of which can only end in tears. Habits like drowning all your sorrows induced by the previous habits. All these habits, and many more, have their roots in gender identity, which in turn is based on the belief that 'I am my body'. Not a good idea. Not happy-making ideas. Perhaps it's just as well you are just pretending!

Gender Liberation

The gender belief is one of the most potent beliefs that sustains the feeling of being trapped. If you can throw off this idea, because ultimately it's just an idea, you will feel a real sense of liberation. Not just from a false identity, but from all the external messages aimed at 'hooking onto' your gender belief. All gender-focussed marketing ceases to have any power over you. It becomes a laughable attempt to capture you and then your money. And when you can laugh and not worry in the face of gender-based marketing, when you can see through it, you are free of a false pretence. It's not a question of denying the gender of your body, simply ceasing to identify with it. Ceasing to say, "I am my gender"' Ceasing to pretend you are a girl or a boy. That will happen naturally when you realise that you are no what you see in the bathroom mirror in the morning!

The Third Pretend

"I am what I look like!"

Afraid Not!

It naturally follows that, if you are not your form or gender you are also therefore not what you look like. You are not your face, pretty or otherwise. You are not your shape, slim, fat or otherwise. When your self-esteem becomes intertwined with the physical image of the face and body it becomes the perfect recipe for much anxiety and a sense of diminishing self worth. From the moment we arrive and hear words such as 'pretty baby', 'what a beautiful little girl', 'what a handsome little boy', many if not most of us will become 'looks-conscious'. We will strive to look good for others in order to attract attention and solicit approval.

Neediness and people-pleasing follow fast, and the craving for continuous confirmation, that we are looking good, becomes a habit that can stay with us for the rest of our life. If our body is not that pretty in the mirror of society's norms, we will go to extraordinary lengths to make it so. Even if it is almost perfect, still we will be encouraged to see deficiencies that need to be fixed. A variety of wipe ons, roll ons, brush ons, spray ons and slap ons will be made available, and will start to gather in all corners of our home. Wardrobes, cupboards and drawers will fill with the latest cut, the 'in look', what's hot and what makesyalooksogooood! All because we identify with how our face and body appears to others.

The good news is old news. Beauty is much deeper than the skin. It doesn't appear in curves or complexions, it doesn't show up as shape, eye shadow or a washboard six pack. Beauty comes, as we all know, from a deeper place within. It doesn't even come *from* personality or character, it comes *through* character. It is the very nature of the self, of every self, because every self is beautiful. It is not a beauty that has an opposite called ugly. It is real beauty. It is the soul's most natural 'product'. It is felt not seen, sensed and not measured. You know it when it touches you. It's that moment when you walk away from a special encounter with another person. Usually an old and wrinkly-faced person, filled with a lifetime's wisdom and the serenity, that puts you instantly at ease and, as they share themselves with an almost tangible love, you walk away saying, "Weren't they just a beautiful person". Or it strikes you when you least expect it as someone does something utterly, profoundly, selflessly generous and you say, "Wasn't that just a beautiful thing to do?"

Real beauty is what love is. And what love is cannot be seen with physical eyes or touched with physical hands. It cannot be bought, boxed or batched on a production line. Only what love 'does' can be seen and recorded by memory. Believing you are, and pretending to be, what you look like is to lose your connection with love, with your heart, with your 'self'. Not a good idea but a prevalent mistake. Dressing up, making up or building up your form and then pretending to be beautiful is no substitute for the natural beauty that needs no pretence.

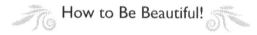 How to Be Beautiful!

It sounds like a good book title and I'm surprised no-one has written it yet. In truth, it could only be about 'truth', simply because the deepest truths are beautiful. It has been said that truth is beauty and beauty is truth. So what is truth? It is that which is real and that which is real is that which never changes. That which is eternal. That which is untouched by time and decay. Sit quietly, allow the world out there to disappear from your awareness for a few moments. Allow all thoughts to fade, all feelings to dissolve, all memories to evaporate, and what is left? Just you, just the 'I' that says 'I am'. And then, just in that moment, you will know the true you. And it will be something beautiful to behold, but you cannot hold it. In that moment, you will see and know that everything that is not you is subject to change and decay, and therefore not so beautiful. You will intuitively sense that only you are that which is real, and that all else is unreal…but fun. From the awareness of that truth, from he beauty that love is, will emerge the creation of something beautiful, such as your own serenity amidst the chaos we call living.

The Fourth Pretend

"I am my Nationality"

Definitely not

Walk down any canning factory and you will see the part of the process where the label is stuck on the tin. Nationality is similar, only slower! Down through history, certain people decided to label certain bits of land or territory with certain 'name labels'. If you are born on any of those bits of land, then you were automatically labelled with the same label as the land. 'Apparently' that makes you a different human being from the other human beings with other labels from other bits of labelled land. You start to pretend to be the label known as nationality. Your identity is lost in the label.

When some people with labels from other labelled territories enter the room, you might ignore them or fight them simply judge them as inferior because they have a different label. Which is like saying one can of beans in tomato sauce is much better than the other because it's label is brighter in colour.

There are now over 180 national label types for human beings throughout the world. It's no wonder there is so much division, fragmentation, separation and therefore inter-national conflict. But are you a label? Is that what you are? Obviously not. It's just an idea. But we pretend we are our nationality and then we build histories, cultures, customs and traditions around the labels. Arrogance emerges when we consider 'our' country/culture being the best and others judged as inferior or a threat.

A nationality is nothing more than a concept. It exists only in the mind. Yes, languages are different, but they are just physical sounds, physical symbols made of physical noise that emerge from the physical body. And those sounds have simply developed in different physical ways. The real language of human beings is the language of love. Not Hollywood love, but the love that creates unity between people and not division. It's a language that transcends labels. It connects and unites human beings. That's why it's impossible for any human to give love to another when they identify with 'my label' and see 'your label' as different and lesser. National identity is simply a 'game of separation' sustained by those who seek to control the behaviours and therefore the destinies of others. The culture of control has a long tradition. Love is ignorant of national labels, because love sees no division, no separation, no barriers anywhere or anytime.

While your body can be covered with labels (especially after a trip to the clothes store!), 'you' cannot be labelled. What cannot be seen cannot be labelled which means identified. Yes some may say you are a 'nasty person' or you are a 'fabulous friend', but these are just labels for your personality and you are not your personality. You create your personality, but it's not what you are, not what the I that says 'I am' is. Personality is made up of all the tendencies, traits and habits that you have created in your life so far. But as the creator you are not your creation. You are not your personality. Personality comes from the word 'persona', which means mask. And you are not a mask. You create and wear a mask. Some of us create various personality masks, which is why we sometimes feel and act differently with different people. It just means our sense of self, our identity, is lost in our personality in much the same way that some actors get lost in the character they play, or some artists get lost in their own paintings. Some artists even say, "I am my painting". Not possible!

 Imagine a World

Imagine a world where there are no labels on anyone or anything any more. Would it be a divided world or a united world? Would it be a conflicted world or a harmonious world? Imagine a world where all labelling had disappeared from all conversations. Would we say more or less? How much more or less? What would we use to fill the gaps? Imagine a world where whenever you referred to a label, people would chuckle and say, "He hasn't got it yet, the penny hasn't dropped…yet. He still sees labels". Would you feel embarrassed or appreciative that they reminded you? Would you be able to still hold a conversation with no reference whatsoever to labels? If so, what would you talk about? Try it today. And you will become acutely aware of how much 'labelling' dominates your perceptions and thoughts about your self and others.

The Fifth Pretend

"I am my Religion"

Absolutely Impossible

Any religion is based on a set of specific beliefs. It is a belief system created by other people sometime in the past and then recorded and 'represented' by symbols, called words, which are handed down from one generation to the next.

You are born into a body not into a belief system. You are not born into a set of ideas and concepts. You are not born into other peoples beliefs and perceptions. Your body did not come out of the womb of your physical mother with Christian or Muslim or Buddhist stamped on the forehead. All beliefs are learned or assimilated. They are 'programmed in' by someone else, usually parents or, in the case of religious beliefs, the local priest/ minister/imam. These beliefs are not what YOU are, regardless of how right they may sound.

Can you change your beliefs? Of course you can. You may have believed the earth was flat and then one day you saw a picture that showed it be round and so you changed your belief about the earth. Who did the changing? You did. So follow the logic, if not your experience. There is you, and then there are your beliefs. So you are not your beliefs. You don't have to believe anything. You don't need to pretend you are your beliefs! As soon as you adhere to a set of beliefs you start to identify your self with them. You will likely believe you are right in your belief. You therefore start to believe that if others beliefs are different they are wrong. You separate your self and close your self to other beliefs, and to the holders of those other beliefs. And then you perceive them as a threat. Some people will go to war in order to defend and justify 'my beliefs' which they believe is what 'I am'.

This is why, to an enlightened soul, there can never be a good reason to go to war. It's just two sides who have lost their identity in a different set of beliefs.

So deep is the habit of identifying with a set of beliefs it's hard to shake off this false identity. So many other things accompany and grow out of pretending to be a belief system! Things like daily rituals, uniforms, power over others, righteous arrogance, barriers going up that are created to stop others beliefs 'getting in' and corrupting 'our' belief system, guilt when we create the slightest doubt about our learned beliefs, the intention to cajole and convert others to believe the same thing.

But you may be thinking now, "Well all that is just 'your' belief", to which I frequently reply and reiterate here , "You mustn't believe a word I say. But don't not believe either! Look for yourself. See for your self."   To believe blindly is to avoid looking and seeing for your self.

When you do see the folly of just believing what others say or have said, what others expound in books and scriptures, you stand at the edge of the territory within you, within your consciousness, that is beyond belief. Otherwise known as 'knowing'. When you 'know' then you no longer need to believe. When you see your self as you really are, when you feel your peace and know that peace is your nature, then beliefs are unnecessary. Now you know.

But perhaps you believe that you have to have some beliefs. Some say, "I have to have an opinion". Do you? Or is it just another prevalent belief that keeps you under a self inflicted pressure to 'have an opinion'. Do you have to have, or do, anything?   Don't think so. Try a day without opinions and notice how present, how peaceful and how positive you are. Listen to yourself and you will quickly hear what you believe. Watch what comes up when you express your beliefs. Notice how you feel certain emotions like anxiety, irritation and sadness most frequently when you forcefully articulate your beliefs. Notice how you go on the defensive when you hear others beliefs that do not concur with yours.

These are all signals that you are trapped in a prison cell of your own making. The bars are your beliefs. The lock on the door is your apparent certainty that 'I am right'. But that's just another belief. And the door is closed, which means you are closed. And when you lock yourself in, when you are closed to others and the world around you, your only companion is misery. But even then you will likely have learned to believe that some misery is natural and necessary to the grand struggle called living. Is this non-sense, or just nonsense, or both?

Who's Right or Wrong?

Trying to prove, justify, and impose your beliefs is not a pleasant way to live. Conflict is always round the corner, there's always a hidden tension in every conversation. You can keep on living with that tension, as most do. Some even turn it into a living! They are sometimes called journalists! But if you prefer to relax and find a little peace in the world, you probably already know it's time to let go. It's quite easy really. Let's say we both look at the same tree. You describe what you see, how the tree looks to you. Then I describe how the tree looks to me. Both perceptions are bound to be different to some degree or other. The degree itself doesn't matter. They are different because we both look from different angles, different points of viewing. So who has the right view? Neither. Both are right from their point of view. And it's totally useless to try to convince the other. Which is why we don't when looking at trees...mostly! It's just the same for any beliefs, because what is a belief but a 'frozen perception' that is crystalized at one moment in the past and then preserved in the archives of your consciousness. The attempted imposition of our beliefs upon others is just a way of trying to control others, which is another of life's impossibilities. Yet most of us will learn to believe it is not only possible to control others but that it is a necessity! You have to have some compassion for those that identify with the label 'politician' here, simply because they live their lives believing that it's their job to manipulate other's points of view and therefore their beliefs. It's a belief in an impossible mission that is guaranteed to generate much stress, not to mention the occasional exercise in what we have come to know as 'spin'.

The Sixth Pretend

"I Am what I do"

Wrong again!

Do you ever have trouble leaving work at work? Do you ever take work home, not in your briefcase, but in your head? Is your mind just as busy at home thinking about work as it is at work? It simply means you have invested your identity in what you do or what you have done. You are pretending to be what you do. It's a common mistake in our super busy world full of super busy people doing what they believe are super important things. It just means that they, and perhaps you, have not yet learned that you are not what you do.

Let's say you are an architect. Many acquaintances over the years have also told you they think you are a great architect, and you believed them. Then one day someone comes along and says, "Did you really build that rubbish down at end of the road." How do you feel? If not devastated, then somewhat sad. Then the sadness turns to anger and indignation. And the next time you see the same person you say, "Sorry, can't stop to talk now, got to go," because you are afraid they might say the same again or something similar.

So what did you do? You created three moments of suffering for your self – sadness, anger and fear. Why, because you believe you are an architect. But is architect what you are or what you do? It's what you do. But you learned to believe it is what you are. You learned to identify your self with what you do. This then becomes the root cause of your entirely self-created emotional pain. If you were not identified with what you do you would not react emotionally. You might be able to say, "That's an interesting perception. What particularly don't you like about it? I'd be interested to know for similar projects I might do in the future". Or something to that effect. No suffering. No pain. No emotional reaction, just a cool and measured response - because you don't identify your self with what you do.

Essentially what we 'do' is just a role, or one of many roles we play. Ask any actor and they will tell you they are not the roles they play. They will remind you of the danger in identifying with the role, of pretending to be the role offstage. They will remind you that you play many roles on the stage of life and that if you get stuck in one or two roles, which is what tends to happen for most of us (conditioning again), then creativity and playfulness will leave your life and you will start to take things far too seriously. Sound familiar?

Most seriousness is based on identifying with one or two roles, usually one at home and one at work. Behind all seriousness is fear in one of its many forms. And fear is not only stress, it's a sign that love is absent. It's an emotion that prevents you from accepting and appreciating others. It's a signal that you have closed your self around an idea of what you do and you are identifying your self with that idea. Whenever things turn a little serious in your day-to-day life take a moment to reflect and it's likely you will see you are pretending 'to be' what you do!

So What ARE You Worth?

Do you find you think a lot about your position, pay, possessions and privileges in your life? If you do, you are almost certainly basing your self-worth and self-esteem (the value you place upon your self) on something entirely transient, superficial and extremely way beyond your control. This is why you frequently feel anxious and insecure. You perceive much of life 'out there' as a threat. This is why knowing and giving love becomes impossible much of the time. You are so busy 'holding on' to what you believe defines you that you cannot relax within your self. You are too busy feeling 'insecure' to freely give of your self to others. And when you're busy creating all these inner mental tensions, then your heart just shrinks back into itself. If your heart had a mind of it's own it would probably say to you, "Let me know when your done with all your little fears, when you are tired of all your worries, exhausted by all that 'holding on' to what you are using to define your worth, and I will be here to embrace you with so much love that you will wonder why you ever ignored me in the first place." Or something to that effect!

The Seventh Pretend

"I am my Position"

Unfortunately Not!

The moment you identify with a position, whether it's in an organisation or a community, or even within your family, either a superiority complex or an inferiority mindset is likely to kick in. If you identify your self with a higher position than others, if you look down on others in any way, others will sense your arrogance and start to keep their distance. If you identify with an inferior position in relation to others, whether it appears as a formal title or just as your mindset, then subservience and neediness are likely to emerge in your behaviour. Others are likely to either attempt to take advantage of you or ignore you. But if you do not identify with a position, whether it's a formal or informal position, then you are more likely to see others as equals and act with a certain acceptance, humility and grace, which will tend to attract the same in return.

This is not easy because we believe position is synonymous with power. We believe power over others comes with position. Roughly translated that means we believe that we can control others. But we don't, we can't , it's an illusion. You can no more control others than you can stop a running train with your bare hands. Your position may trigger fear in others and it may appear they are motivated by that fear, and so it may appear that you are controlling them. But that's not power, it's not control. It's just an invoked fear of authority, a neat trick often taught by parents and educators, and used in organisations by lazy managers. It's the lazy way to get what you want in a relationship. It only works when the other fears what they believe is a higher authority, or they fear the emotional reaction of someone.

When you identify with your position, when you 'pretend' to be the position, notice how insecure you regularly feel as you perceive threats to your position. When we believe we are our position we expect to be respected more than usual and in a certain way. When that respect does not come we tend to create anger in the form of resentment. We throw that resentment into the realtionship and then wonder why the relationship stops working and why there is resentment coming the other way!

If you still crave the recognition and respect of others, if you still seek the acceptance and approval of others, it's easy to misuse a position to get it. But recognition, approval and acceptance of others are all traps. Once you start 'taking' these energies a dependency is likely to develop. This neediness will communicate itself through all that you say and do. And as others sense that neediness they may start to exploit it, or simply withhold what you seek in order to satisfy it. And as you react to their withholding they then appear to have power over you. Such are the games we play when we don't know love. Why? Because the root cause of all neediness is a cry for love, and using your position to be recognised and respected is not the route back to authentic love. You want others to make you feel loved because you've not yet realized that you are love. You have not yet realized you are responsible for your feelings. You have not yet realized it's not 'them' that makes you 'feel' accepted and approved, recognised and respected, it's you.

So What Are YOU?

So if you are not your form, not your looks, not your position, not your religion, then that leaves one simple question. Who are YOU? The simple answer is the 'I' that says 'I am'. And it is the 'I' that is aware that it is the 'I' that says 'I am' so the 'I' is awareness. You and I are aware that we are aware so we are awareness. You and I are awareness itself. And when you become aware that you are awareness then you become aware that everything that is 'in' your awareness is what you are not. And as you realise that you are not any thing that's in your awareness you come to know your self as ... awareness. If you practice this awareness, of being only awareness, it is a little challenging at first. That's because you are so accustomed to identifying with what is 'in' your awareness. But gradually you will begin to 'see' and know your self as you are, as pure awareness. You will then start to see everything else as the 'content' of awareness. And the more you notice that you are not the content of awareness the more frequently and lastingly will you be content.

The Birth of Our Oldest and Dearest Companion

All these misidentifications are not the only myths or illusions that we create about our identity. They are not the only ways we pretend to be something that we are not without realising that we are 'pretenders'. They are seven of many, perhaps the most frequent seven, the most obvious seven. Each and every day we all misidentify with hundreds of things and don't notice we are doing so. This is why we forget that love is what we are and how we lose our capacity to be loving in our relationships with others. This is also how our oldest and dearest companion, our ego, takes birth, stays alive and remains by our side. The ego, contrary to some popular opinions is not the driving force of your life. It is not the sum total of your values and beliefs. It is not 'the self', though it does seem so sometimes. The ego is the only real enemy in your life. It kills your happiness, your creativity and your capacity to relate well with others.

All personal development programmes and processes, all relationship guidance and counselling, all spiritual endeavours and mental disciplines in the world will make little difference to the quality of your life or the contentment of your being until you are free of your oldest and closest companion. And yet, as we shall see, it is not even real. The ego's unreality lies at the root of all our suffering because it is based on a lie. See the lie, stop sustaining the lie, and suffering will be no more. Understand the ego and you will understand almost everything.

Sit back and buckle up as we ride into the endarkened world of ghosts and phantoms. Into the place where all pretending has its origins. What follows is an opportunity to see:
- who you really are behind all those false identities,
- why you keep feeling what you keep feeling but would rather not feel
- how you can free yourself from all emotional turbulence if you choose to be free
- how to consciously be your your original, authentic and beautiful self... again.

It's been a long time since you were your self. And yet, no time at all!

The EGO

It's only relatively recently that a fresh wave of writers and teachers have come on stream with attempts to clarify and expose the ego's existence and its effect on both our personal well-being and our mutual coexistence. All still differ slightly, and a few not so slightly, on what exactly the ego is. But on one thing almost all agree. Ego is the enemy of awakening, of self realisation. And yet it is not the enemy because ultimately it is not real. The main reason why there is no absolute consensus on what the ego is seems to be the lack consensus about what consciousness is, what the mind is, what the intellect is, what conscience is and how these 'faculties' of consciousness, of the self, interrelate and interact.

If you have already investigated and explored the nature and workings of consciousness, of your self, you will already know that words and terms are only descriptions, signposts and pointers at best, and not what they point to. The map is not the territory as they say. But it is still easy to get stuck discussing the map as if it were the territory. As we enter the territory of consciousness, as we explore the meaning of ideas like intuition, mind, memory, emotions and feelings, I recommend that you adopt the mindset of a curious and enthusiastic researcher exploring a dense jungle before the film crew arrive to make the documentary about life in the rainforest. See if you can see within the jungle of your consciousness what I describe in words and concepts.

Every time you see for your self, within your self what is described here, find a way of taking note. Perhaps a tick in the margin. If you cannot see what is described, perhaps a question mark that you can return to later, and then move on. But if something is not clear, just before you do move on, please take the smallest of moments and see if you feel any resistance to what I am describing. If you do then it's not that you can't see what I describe, but more likely you don't want to see it. You may also see that the presence of any resistance means the ego is at work. It's holding shut the gate to make sure you don't discover a new reality in which 'it' is no longer required. Acknowledge the resistance, smile knowingly at the resistance and then move on. Finally, I recommend you don't read on if you are tired in any way. Wait until you are refreshed and focused.

We start with a definition and a description of our old friend… the ego. I invite you to take a moment to reflect. Put aside any other definitions you have read or encountered in the past. Close the book for a second or find a blank space somewhere at the back and write down your definition or description of the ego. This is to get you in the mood, in the groove, looking inwards while you are looking outwards…so to speak. How would you define the ego – write it down. There is no right answer, just your answer, as you see it now.

When you have finished reflecting and writing return to this page.

Defining and Describing the EGO

In seminars and retreats, all manner of ideas and insights tend to emerge from the group as definitions and perceptions of the ego vary. Concepts such as beliefs, thoughts, feelings, values, esteem, image, self-perception, even personality, are a few of the components that people believe make up the ego. It is commonly seen as the 'driving force' of our life and the word that comes up most is, of course, the 'self'. Here is a definition and a description that I'd like to work with. It's not carved in stone, and if it doesn't work for you then you can throw it out at the end of the book! In this definition I am also describing how the ego is formed within consciousness.

**Ego is attachment to the wrong image
of my 'self' or belief about my 'self'.**

And then just expanding that a little

**EGO is the 'self' (the 'I' that says 'I am') attaching itself
to an image or to a belief
which I then mistake for my self.**

If you are 'self aware' in the moment you become attached to any thing, then you will also 'notice' three things
1. the attachment 'happens' within your consciousness
2. you lose your sense of 'identity' in the 'image' of the object of attachment which you create on the screen of your mind.
3. that 'image' can be of an object, or an idea, or a memory or a belief.

Therefore

**EGO is the self (the 'I') attaching to
and IDENTIFYING with an image
that is not the self**

This takes place entirely within consciousness, within the self, on the screen of the mind. You are not your mind. The mind is in you, in consciousness, but the 'I' is not the mind. We do this hundreds of times every day but we are not aware of it. For example, let's say you are driving past the local BMW dealership and you see the new model has arrived. You think to myself, "Yes please. I'll have one of those." You return three weeks later with the money and there you are in your new BMW. As you drive down the road you pass some friends. As you pass them, you are saying through your eyes and through the smile on your face, "Hey look at me, no don't look at me, look at the car, look at the car!". In that moment you want them to see the car but with you in it. You want them to see you as the car, the car as a symbol of you. The image you are projecting to them of your self is BMW. In that moment, you are not only 'attached' to the car, your 'identity' is invested in the car.

This is easily proved, because all someone (lets call him Mr. Scratcher) has to do is walk up to your new BMW, run a coin down the paintwork and how do you feel? A little upset? A small amount of anger? You perceive their behaviour as outrageous so there is the birth of rage. You are in a state of pleasure or pain? You are in pain. Who creates your pain, your anger? You do. It's not Mr. Scratcher that creates your suffering towards his actions, it's you. He just does his scratching bit with the coin down the paintwork. So, from a rational point of view, he scratches your car and you feel pain, which means YOU THINK YOU ARE A CAR! In that moment you are under the illusion that you are a car. Obviously at that moment you are not 'aware' that you are identifying your self with a car. You are just angry.

We all make this same mistake within our consciousness many times every day with different objects, people, ideas, beliefs etc. This is why the simplest definition of ego is that it's a 'mistake'. We mistake our self for some thing that we are not.

In order to see exactly *how* we do this, we need to go *where* we do this, which is within our consciousness. Consciousness is simply the energy of the self and, within the energy field of your consciousness, you have a faculty known as a mind. Everyone has a mind. The mind is like a screen. It is the arena of creation where you, the creator, create. You can create anything you want on the screen of your mind. And you do – thoughts, images, ideas, concepts, symbols, memories – you can put any of these up on the screen of your mind at any moment.

As the proud owner of a new BMW, you are standing looking at your BMW as it sits outside on the road. You bring the image of the car in through your physical eyes, and you put that image up on the screen of your mind. No problem there, as you have to think about the car, put petrol in it, wash it, etc. But the mistake begins when 'you' leave the center of your consciousness, and you, the 'I' that says 'I am', go into your mind. Not only that, but you go into the image of the car on the screen of your mind. You lose your sense of 'I', your sense of 'self', in the image of the car that's on your mind. This is called 'attachment'.

Along comes Mr. Scratcher who runs a coin down the side of your brand new car and what do you feel. Much anger. Much pain. Why? Because not only are you attached to the car, you are effectively identified with the car. You've lost your 'sense of self' in the image of the car that you created on the screen of your mind. So when Mr. Scratcher touches the car 'out there' it's 'as if he touches you. Which is obviously nonsense. You are not a car. And he doesn't touch you. But your angry reaction indicates that you think you are the car because you take Mr. Scratcher's action very personally.

So if you don't want the pain, if you don't want the anger, if you don't want to suffer, it's simple, don't get attached to the car. Don't lose your sense of self in the image of the car on the screen of your mind. In other words, remain detached, which means that, if the car is scratched or damaged in any way, it's not a problem, you don't react, you don't create emotional pain. Can you see it?

It sounds simple in theory, but in reality it's obviously not. While we all learn to start 'attaching' to things as children we are not aware that we do so. No-one teaches us the consequences of attachment at a mental and emotional level. No-one explains the mechanics of our consciousness. Although it's not easy to 'see' at first, this inner process of attaching ones self to an image and misidentifying with that image is the root cause of ALL mental/emotional suffering. If you can see this mechanism, if you can be aware of what you are doing within your consciousness when you 'attach', if you can see this 'mistake', then you stand on the threshold of restoring true freedom and therefore authentic happiness to your life. Why? Because the root of ALL unhappiness, all suffering, is this same mistake that we all make in different ways (ie. attachment to different images) within our consciousness. We sacrifice our freedom the moment we attach our self to anything.

Only when you take the time to stop and look, not just read, but stop, reflect, become aware of what you are doing within your consciousness, your self, and see for your self, will you clearly see the frequency of mistaking your self for something that you are not. Only when you take your attention away from the world 'out there' and pay some attention to how you create the world 'out there' as images 'in here', on the screen of your mind, that you start to see your habitual attachment. Only then can you slowly but surely set your self free. Many more examples to come and to play with, so stay with me.

Naturally Unnatural

A frequent question at this point is, "Surely anger, and therefore pain, is a natural response to someone damaging your car or your property?"

Any suffering on any level actually means something is 'unnatural'. It means something is out of balance, out of harmony within you, within your own consciousness. And only you can fix it, because only you create it. But in the moment that you find yourself angry or fearful the last thing you are able to see and acknowledge is that YOU are the creator of your anger/fear because YOU have attached your self and misidentified yourself with something that you are not.

Perhaps you are thinking, "But surely it's OK, it's natural, to suffer when such things happen in life?" It's a prevalent belief to which many are attached in the world today. But if we say mental and emotional pain is OK, then the equivalent at a physical level would be consciously sticking a knife in your leg. Not many people 'choose' to do that every day.

Perhaps you cannot yet see that you have the power to choose what you will feel in response to any event. If so that means you have not quite yet realized that you are one hundred percent responsible for all your emotions, for all your feelings. In other words, you still 'believe' it's Mr.

Scratcher with the coin that is creating your anger/pain. You have not yet realized that you are responsible for your anger, your suffering... always. It is entirely you, because it's your response, and only you are responsible for your responses.

Perhaps you are thinking that it's not the car that is the problem here. It's the time and all the money that it's taken to buy the car. If so then your attachment is not to the image of the car but to the image of the money or the mental story of all the time you spent to get the money to get the car. It's the same inner process or mechanism within your consciousness, just a different image you are attached to and identifying with.

Perhaps it's not the car or the money that is the issue, but you get upset because you now have to spend time getting the car fixed. Then the image you are attached to and identifying with is using your time to do something else. And because of this scratching incident you now have to do something you did not want to do. It's as if you have 'lost', been denied, what you wanted to do. It's the same suffering but a different image that you are attached to. If you were not attached to doing something else with your time, if you were detached, then you would be flexible and free to go with the flow that life brings to you. In this case you would switch time and attention to getting the car fixed without complaint, without suffering. After all, you already know that 'stuff happens'. That's the nature of life on planet Earth!

Or perhaps it's not the car or the money or the time that is the issue, but it's a matter of 'respect'. By damaging your car, you believe someone has shown such disrespect towards you, and perhaps towards society. Then the image you are attached to is of being a highly respected person and of others giving you respect. But if you drop your attachment to the image of always being respected, if you no longer have a 'neediness' for the respect of others to bolster your self-respect, then there is no suffering, no pain. When people do not give you respect you are able to move on with ease, without the loss of your peace, your power or your happiness. Or are you needy of the recognition and respect from others? If so then, in truth, it's not 'you' that is needy but the ego.

Perhaps you are also now thinking that I am saying that you should just roll over when someone damages your property and do and say nothing. However that is not what detachment means. Let's say the car is now damaged, how will you respond to that. You have choices. If Mr Scratcher is still there you might say, "I take it you will pay for the damage you have done." Or you could just call the police as the law has been broken. But normally with such incidents people scratch and run.

So what are your choices a) you could pay for the scratch to be fixed b) you could get the insurance to pay for it c) you could just leave the scratch as it is and continue to use the car or d) you could sell the car with the scratch on it.

You always have choices. Why can you not 'create' these possible ways forward? Why can you not be creative? Because your consciousness is filled with the emotion of anger. And you cannot be creative when you are scared or angry. The emotion, that you create, is a form of self sabotage, as it kills your creative capacity. Fortunately it's temporary, as is all emotion, so it must pass. Being detached doesn't mean that you don't care about the car, or that you don't value the car. But as we will see attachment is not the same as caring and while attachment is often confused with valuing it's not possible to 'ascribe value' to anything as long as you are attached to it.

The scratched car is just one example. For many people a scratched car is never an issue. For them, it might be other things, other objects, like the new carpet. Perhaps you've just had a new carpet delivered. You are so happy with your new carpet but it's not long after the dinner guests arrive and you can see coffee spilling over the edge of a cup and making its way down to the carpet, as if in slow motion! You cry out in pain, "Aargh, my new carpet!" In that moment you are a carpet. In that moment, you forget one of the most important formulas in life which goes something like this. Carpet plus gravity plus coffee equals stain. Car plus violent people plus roadside parking equals scratched cars. Which all adds up to the enlightening realisation that carpets are designed to catch falling coffee and cars are designed to be scratched. That's life!

Going to Extremes

What if we take this to its most extreme, what if it's your child that is damaged. Surely we are not meant to be detached. Surely you cannot be detached if that happens. Would that not mean we don't care? It's also a frequent question in seminars and retreats.

The answer is the same, the mechanism within consciousness is the same. It's just harder to see and apply, because the deepest attachments that we form are to our own family. Let's say your child is badly hurt by the violence of another person. How would you feel? How would most people feel? Somewhere between sad, hurt and angry, with 'the angry' outlasting the other two emotions and probably escalating. So it's as if you are suffering too. And what does the child need at that moment? Empathy, care, compassion, support and your clarity of mind to see and perhaps make a quick and important decision like, "Hospital, now!"

But if you are suffering, you cannot give care, support, clarity etc. Actually you are now the one in need of the very same things, because

It's Not Academic

The subjects of love, ego and emotion cannot be left to the experts, because there are no experts. Love is not an academic subject that you can study in the cloisters of an educational institution. These are places where we affirm and rely on those whom we deem to be authorities on matters in which we believe we need to be educated. But the housewife or mechanic, who have been meditating and exploring their spirituality for some years, are more likely to have a clearer insight into love than many university professors. The earnest seeker, attempting to understand why they are suffering so much, are just as likely to have a clearer insight into the formation and the mechanics of the ego than the psychiatric consultant with BSc in psychology. Ultimately the only authority on matters of love, ego and emotion is you. The laboratory in which you do your research is you. The methodology is meditation, contemplation and silent reflection upon what is happening ...within you!

you are suffering yourself. Someone who is emotionally suffering cannot effectively help another who is suffering. Even an attempt to bandage a wound will be less than your best possible effort if you are emotionally devastated or enraged.

Detachment is a word that, for many, has come to mean cold, distant and unloving. But it doesn't mean that, it just means you don't suffer when others suffer. It means you do not identify with the suffering of another. It means you don't descend into emotional turmoil with them. It means you are able to stay calm, strong and fully available to see and create the most appropriate response to the others pain, and to meet their need in that moment. When you do 'react' emotionally to the suffering of another it means you are attaching to, and identifying with, the image of their suffering, that you are creating in your mind. You are mistaking your self for their pain! It's just egos little game.

While we learn to become easily attached to external things like positions, power, pay, privileges, other people and their pain, they are all, in reality, not outside your self in the moment of attachment. They are images or concepts that we create on the screen of our mind.

We also easily attach to and identify with things like ideas, memories and, most commonly, our beliefs. Do you ever argue? When you argue, it means you have an opinion and, at the core of your opinion, is your belief. When you hear the other person's opinion, which is in contradiction to yours, you perceive their belief as a threat, not just to your belief, but to you personally. Why? Because not only are you attached to your belief, but you identify your self with it. In that moment it's as if you are that belief. An argument ensues which can become quite heated. Heat is a sign that you are suffering again. Heatedness is the sign of emotion, usually some form of anger. But are you your beliefs, is that what you are? Can you change your beliefs? Of course you can. So who does the changing? You do. So there is you, and then there are your beliefs. So you are not your beliefs.

One sure way to disarm your self and the other before an argument erupts is simply to say, "That's interesting, I can see why you might believe that. Personally I don't, I have a different point of view. But tell me more about your point of view on this." In the moment you detach and stop identifying with your belief, the heat is gone, your resistance towards their belief dissolves and normal communication is restored. It works every time. You only have to detach your self from the belief you are creating and sustaining in your mind. Unless of course you are one of those people who likes to provoke an argument, so that you have an excuse to get angry (emotional) so that you can satisfy your emotional addiction. More about that later.

Understanding the ego and how you create it allows you to understand why people do what they do, why they behave in certain ways, why you behave in certain ways, especially in moments when you 'react' as opposed to respond.

Where there is **EGO** there is **ATTACHMENT**

Where there is **ATTACHMENT** there is **RESISTANCE**

Where there is **RESISTANCE** there is **FEAR**

So to complete the circle, wherever or whenever there is **FEAR,** there is **EGO**

Correcting the Mistake

All fear arises from the ego. So if all stress is fear in one of its many guises, and all ego is just a mistake (mistaken identity), if you want to be free of stress, all you need to do is correct the mistake. At which point you may ask (if you haven't already), what is the right image to attach to and identify with? If ego is attachment to the wrong image, what is the right one?

In truth there is no 'right image', because you are not an image. We are not images, we are beings of consciousness, beings that are consciousness itself. And consciousness has no image. The being of consciousness, the self, is the creator and projector of images. An image is a picture/idea, a 'thing', on the screen of the mind that you create, and you are not a picture/idea or a 'thing' on your mind. This can sound like the opposite of what we are taught, and it is. That's why the way to restore your power, your peace and your happiness, is not by learning something new here but by unlearning what is old. The authentic self has no image. Drop all attachment to any and all images, and you will be your self...again. Stop identifying with some 'thing' that you are not, which includes all 'things', and you will know yourself as love again. This is the purpose of meditation, to see and drop all the images that the self is losing itself in. To restore ones awareness of ones self as...pure awareness!

As long as your energy, your light, is trapped in any 'thing' on your mind you cannot connect accurately, lovingly, with others, you cannot fully flow to others. Love is connection. Love is you flowing outwards towards ,and connecting with, the other and the world. When love flows and connects accurately it means the self is no longer busy attaching to and identifying with something that the 'I' that says "I am' is not! The self is egoless, if only for a few moments to begin with!

Understanding Others

It's hard to see what people are *attached* to because the attaching is happening within their consciousness. It's often hard to see the exact nature of peoples *fear* because we are good at disguising our fears. But you cannot disguise the *behaviour*, which is always some form of *resistance*.

Signs and Symptoms of Attachment and Egos Presence

So what kinds of things do people do when they are scared, when they are under the influence of fear, when they are attached to and identifying with something they are not? What kinds of resistant behaviours would you see during your average day? A short list would include:

Criticizing Complaining, Blaming, Liking, Disliking, Disapproving, Possessing, Envying, Desiring, Projecting, Competing, Controlling, Condescending, Correcting, Doubting, Defending, Judging, Self Limiting, Fragmenting, Escaping, Avoiding, Denying, Lying, Worrying

If you use your own personal experience of behaving in these ways, and go in behind each of these visible behaviours, you can follow a trail back to their origin within your consciousness, within your self, which is the ego. You will see what image/idea/belief you are attaching to and losing your self in on the screen of your mind.

Let's take two specific behaviours and do a Sherlock Holmes as we go in behind the behaviours, see how and why they are happening, and the root attachments (images/ideas/beliefs that we are identifying with) that are causing them.

1. CRITICISING

Example
"I think your idea is not very good, in fact it's a terrible idea, it's the worst idea I've heard and it will never work."

Specific Fear
I think my idea is better and I'm scared your idea will be accepted, so I criticise (attack) your idea.

Identification/Attachment
I am attached to and identified with the IMAGE of my own idea. So I perceive your idea as a threat to my idea and, because I am identified with my idea, I perceive your idea (you) as an attack on me personally. Hence the criticism of your idea, which is an attack on you, which is how I am attempting to defend my idea ie. my self.

Sometimes someone comes up with a new idea and says, "Hey, I have a great idea here. I'll leave it with you, feel free to use it and, if you don't use it, that's OK too. I'm off to get on with the rest of my life and create some more ideas". They are quite detached from their idea. Whereas the person in the above example comes with a very different energy and attitude. They insist that, "MY idea is the best, and it has to be used". The moment they sense that others are not seeing it that way they become prickly and emotionally upset. They suffer. They are stuck.

2. POSSESSING

Example

"I didn't like it when I saw you laughing and obviously having fun with that person at the party last night. You were with them for 22.3 minutes... weren't you? You like them don't you? Are you going to see them again? You're not going to leave me are you? Please don't leave me!"

Specific Fear

I'm scared they might like me less, or even leave me.

Identification/Attachment

Identification with and attachment to the IMAGE of the other person.

Our deepest attachment is almost always to another person. Frequently mistaken for love. Even if we have not yet had the intellectual realisation deep in our bones, as they say, we all know love is not attachment. Have you ever had someone try to possess you. It's as if you sense their attachment, their possessiveness. The first thing you are inclined to do is either push them away or sidestep the relationship. Unless of course you are needy of their attachment to you, which means you are attached to them! So there is mutually inclusive possessiveness! For obvious reasons such relationships are an emotional can of worms. As we have already seen, both giving and receiving authentic love is only possible when there no attachment. A paradox to the modern conditioned mind.

At this point, the question of close family relationships often comes up again, as people find it hard to work with the idea that it's not healthy to be attached to members of one's family, especially to children. The question usually emerges something like this. "So does this mean that, if something happens to my child, I should not react, not get emotional in any way, not be upset? Surely that is the most natural and necessary thing in the world – to be upset and to show you are upset, when your child has been hurt?" This is the relationship that presents the greatest challenge because the attachment to family members, especially if it is your child, is the deepest.

One answer is as follows. See how it sits with you. Remember, the purpose here is to help you see that you have a choice as to how you respond. We are seeking the most effective choice by restoring our awareness of how our choices are created and how they are sabotaged by the ego/attachment.

As we saw earlier, if you, the parent, are also in emotional pain then you cannot give support, care, empathy and you cannot make very creative and clear decisions. You are the one who now needs the support, care and empathy. You cannot give love to those who are in need of love when you are suffering mentally and emotionally. Only detachment can help. Sometimes the child comes out of their suffering first and starts to empathise with the emotionally suffering parent! So the deeper dimension, or the next level to the answer to this question, is likely to be even more challenging.

The reason the parent is in such distress, when something happens to the child is because we believe it is 'MY child'. It's not 'MY child'. In other words, it is not 'true' to say this is MY child. It implies we possess them, that they are possessed or owned by us. They aren't. They are a unique and individual human being, on their own life journey and, as a parent, we have the extraordinary privilege to be a guide, coach, teacher, friend, advisor and parent. We get the chance to create and play many roles and as we play those roles we teach the child to do the same.

However, many parents cannot see that. They see themselves solely as the parent of 'MY child'. They attach to and identify with the child. And so the main role they play for the child is more often just one role, that of supreme controller! And the moment the child does not do what they are meant to in the parent's eyes, then the parent becomes angry, thereby teaching the child a) how to become angry b) anger towards others is good c) that suffering is OK, it's natural and normal. As the child grows it assimilates the assumption that it will be able to control others and that being stressed and suffering as a result is a good thing.

Detachment doesn't mean that you don't care about your child, or whoever the other person to whom you are attached may be. It just means you don't say they are MINE. You acknowledge and respect their individuality. You don't own or possess them. You know that whatever may happen to them, regardless of what they feel, is not happening to you. You can only be there for them when you are fully present within your self, when you are not losing your self in something or someone that you are not. You can only create the most caring and supportive response when you are not losing your self in the images of their pain on the screen of your own mind.

If we were both in the same room now there is a good chance you may say something like, "This is not easy". I would probably reply, "You're absolutely right, it's not easy, if for no other reason than it's the opposite of what most of us have been taught, and definitely the opposite of how the media portrays such relationships". Even though most of the soaps, movies and dramas are really made of various forms of emotional suffering where attachment is rife and the ego is writ large, occasionally there is the 'line' in response to some personal catastrophe which sounds something like, "We have to stay strong...for them". Which basically means detached and emotion free.

So now it's your turn. Just reading this will not really awaken a clear and consistent awareness of this internal process. The most effective way to allow these insights to be 'realized' is by taking retrospective examples from your own life, seeing what happened exactly, and tracing your reactions back to their original cause, to the source, to ego, to the attachment to an image in your mind. Only then will you be able to see what has become a habit, break the habit, and respond differently next time. I recommend that you take the following three behaviours (3, 4 and 5 opposite - complaining, blaming and self limiting) and do what we have just done with the two previous examples. Draw from your own experience and find an example of when you behaved in each of these ways, and then follow the trail back to the ego i.e. the image in your mind that you were attached to and identifying with, prior to the behaviour.

Use the Grid opposite, or close the book and take a piece of paper, draw the grid, then take each behaviour and find an example from your own experience. Ask your self what was the *fear,* what was the *image* you were attached to/identifying with, within your mind.

Behaviour	Example	Specific Fear	Identification/ Attachment (always an image in the mind)
1 Criticizing	"I think your idea is not very good and will never work."	I think my idea is better and I'm scared your idea will be accepted.	Attachment to and identification with the IMAGE of my own idea
2 Possessing	"I didn't like it when I saw you laughing and obviously having fun with that person at the party last night."	I'm scared you might like me less, or even leave me.	Identification with and attachment to the IMAGE of that person - if they die/ go away it will be as if a part of me dies./is lost
3 Complaining			
4 Blaming			
5 Self-limiting			

Refer to the previous examples (criticizing and possessing) above to refresh the sequence of the process if you need to.

Many find this exercise in awareness challenging and sometimes difficult at first. Like anything else, it's just practice. It becomes easier as you become more aware of what you are doing within your consciousness, within your self, where the creation of attachment, fear and the action originates. When you see that all your fears come from *within* you, and that they are created entirely *by* you, suddenly a new choice opens up *for* you. You can choose not to attach, choose not to create fear, choose to be fearless, which means be egoless. Take five minutes every day to reflect on a particular reaction that day and you will quickly start to see exactly why the fear arose.

Lets explore some examples of those three behaviours.

COMPLAINING

Example

You go into a restaurant and the soup is served cold (it's not meant to be) so you start complaining to everyone at the table, "This bloody soup is cold, how dare they serve me cold soup, especially at this price. I'm really upset." You are angry and therefore obviously suffering. Who creates your suffering? You do.

Specific Fear

The fear that you create is simple – you think you will have to eat cold soup. Or you see this as a sign of disrespect and fear that it may continue.

Identification/Attachment

The image that you have created, are attached to and identifying with, entirely in your own mind, is the image of you eating hot soup.

Once again I am not suggesting you just sit back and let the world walk all over you. So what do you do? You request the waiter and say, "Excuse me, the soup is a bit cold, could you heat the soup for me please. Thank you." This is not complaining, this is giving feedback and making a request. But you are not suffering emotionally in the process. That's because you are not attached to and identifying with always getting hot soup. You are sufficiently detached to accept that the universe sometimes shows up with cold soup!

Perhaps at this point you are thinking, "Awe come on, surely it's OK to complain, surely this kind of incident is so small that it's no big deal to get upset?". But don't forget you are suffering emotionally when you complain and you are always the creator of your suffering. It's always ego at work. Would you choose to create suffering if you could see that you had a choice? And even though you may think it's occasionally OK to create little sufferings over minor incidents like cold soup, remember that the big sufferings in life all started as little sufferings in life. All because you were not aware of your self as the creator of your pain.

BLAMING

Example
You blame others for missing a deadline. "It's their fault the report was not done well and on time."

Specific Fear
Others might think it was in some way you fault that the report was not done on time.

Identification/Attachment
You are attached to, and identifying with, an image of your self being Mr/ Miss Perfect Efficiency who never does anything wrong, badly or late.

Obviously blaming is a common behaviour found in most organisations. But sometimes when something goes wrong someone holds up their hand and says, "Yes that was me, I'll accept responsibility for that." The opposite of ego is humility. They had the humility to be honest, so we respect them for their honesty. Their behaviour attracts respect.

It's useful to be aware that, in all such examples, there is never one right answer. It may be different fears and attachments that are giving rise to the 'resistant' behaviours. In the complaining example, it could be that the cold soup is seen as a sign of disrespect, and so the image that we create and identify with, is that of being a highly respected person. Or in the case of blaming, it could be the fear that job security will be threatened, or a pay increase will be threatened, so the fear is loss of job or loss of money, so the attachment/identification is with the image of a future pay rise, or with the present position.

The 'blame game' is often one of our favourite games and it can be found in the microcosm of the workplace and the macrocosm of a nation. Freeing yourself from blaming others is one thing, but then what do you do when someone blames you? First understand them. If they are blaming you it means they are attached, misidentifying and scared. Whatever has happened is now in the past, and can't be changed, But you can help them shift their attention into the future. Notice, that if you become defensive (defending) in the face of their blame, you are now creating fear. If you do, then look for the attachment behind your defensiveness. It's usually connected to your attachment to a reputation in the eyes of others or to you job. In the end no one is to blame but we are all responsible.

SELF LIMITING

Example
I can't learn to drive

Specific Fear
Fear of success (not failure)

Identification/Attachment
Attachment to and identification with the image of being incapable and inadequate.

Self limiting usually begins with the words 'I can't' or 'I am not able/capable'. Sometimes it arises from the fear of failure, but just as often it's the fear of success.

For example, let's say I went skiing when I was eight years old and fell down and hurt my leg. I came to the conclusion that I can't ski. I create a negative image of my self as a 'not skier' and I attach to and identify with that image. Thirty years later, some friends invite me to join them on a skiing holiday and I reply, "I can't ski, so thanks but no thanks , I won't be joining you." The fear here is not failure but success. I am now so comfortable living in the image of being a 'not skier' that to come skiing I would have to make the effort to break out of my comfort zone, which is defined by this image to which I am now attached and identified. You are asking me to be more today than I was yesterday. No thanks, I am attached to the little image of little me and I much prefer to stay in the comfort zone of that image of my smallness that I have created of my self. I am even prepared to be perceived as weak and a failure by others rather than shatter this image of myself as an incapable person.

This truly is a great exercise to do. Make yourself a cappuccino, find a quiet corner, go through all the other 'resistant behaviours' on the list, find a personal example for each, and trace them back to their origins, which is always the ego, always an image on the screen of your mind, that you, the self, has created and have become attached to. You will rapidly begin to understand and discern when and why are frightened, why they are frightened and why it is ALWAYS because they are attached to an image on their mind, and ALWAYS because they are losing their identity in that image. You will clearly see this process within yourself, and when you do you will know the root cause of many of the feelings and behaviours you'd rather not feel and do! You are then able to make a different choice as to how you respond. As you do you are effectively empowering your self to make the shift from reacting to responding.

When you see the cause of a disease, you can get rid of it forever, but if you only deal with the symptoms of the disease, it just finds other ways to make itself known. Ego is the root of ALL mental/emotional suffering, everywhere, at every moment, at ALL times. It's that dis-ease, within our consciousness, which then finds its way into our thoughts, feelings, words and behaviours. And very often it creates disease within our body. (Some would argue that all physical disease has its origins in the ego). But the ego is just a mistake. A habitual mistake. And like all habits it can be changed. Like any recurring mistake, it can be corrected.

What Difference Does It Make?

Let's say David walks in the room to join our meeting. He starts criticizing everyone on the team. He's been doing this for some weeks now. You are the team leader and all the rest of the team are getting fed up with David so they come to you and start complaining about David's continual criticizing. They ask you to sort him out, because you are the team leader. So you go to David and start saying (as if wagging your finger at him), "You are such a critical person, you shouldn't be criticizing, people are fed up with your criticizing, now stop your criticizing". By which time you are getting quite upset yourself. But wait a minute, what's really happening here, what are you doing? You are criticizing David for criticizing others. You are doing exactly what he is doing. You're suffering as well.

However, now you are a little more enlightened. Now you know that David is criticizing because, behind his criticizing behaviour he is in a state of resistance towards the team. Why? Because he is scared. He is in a state of fear. He's in emotional pain.

When your body is in pain and you go to a doctor, does the doctor lie you down and say, "Well I'm afraid there is a lot of pain here so I will have to put you down (like an old pet dog)"? No, he seeks to understand the cause of the physical pain and help your body to heal. David is not in physical pain, he is in emotional and mental pain. What is the human response to someone who is in pain? It's not condemnation or criticism, it's compassion. So you make one of the biggest shifts you can possibly make in the context of your relationships, from condemnation to compassion. Which is the shift from *fear* to *love*.

Look around the world today and it seems that some days almost everyone is judging, criticising and condemning others. Conflict either precedes or proceeds from such behaviours, and much suffering arises. Perhaps the world is waiting for those who can make this shift from condemnation to compassion. From seeing and *reacting* from fear and anger, to seeing and *responding* from love. Compassion is an act of love. Why are so few making this shift? Because so few are aware and understand the real internal cause of their urge to criticise and condemn. So few understand why it's so hard to generate compassion. And that's because so few really understand the mechanism of ego and how it distorts our perceptions, perspectives and ultimately our behaviour. It's just not a part of our education...yet.

So now you know David is criticizing others because he is suffering and his suffering is called fear. You also know that, behind the fear, he is attached to, and identifying with, some image he is creating in his own mind. Does David know what that is? Probably not, because he is not that self-aware. Do you know what that attachment is? Highly unlikely because you cannot be in someone else's head. So what can you do? How can you help David out of his self-created suffering? Can you 'make' someone change? No. Not possible. So what can you do for David? Two things. First, ask questions. Open ended questions that invite David to explain what is going on in his mind. Questions like, "Is there something bothering you about the team? What's making you uncomfortable? What do you think is making you critical?" As you do, and as he expresses what he is thinking and feeling, he raises his *self-awareness* and begins to see he is entirely *responsible* for his suffering and therefore his behaviour. During such a conversation he is more likely to see and realize exactly what he is attached to, and therefore more likely and able to 'let go'. And that's all detachment is, letting go.

The second way to help David is to remember there is only one way to lead in life, and that is by example. Which makes us all potential leaders. And that means you never ever, ever, ever, criticize anyone... ever. That's easy isn't it? Now you know that if you criticize/condemn anyone it means you are in fear, you are suffering, because you are attached and identified with an image in your mind. It's your ego. This is obviously why we need to be able to see and make changes within our own consciousness before we can be available and fully effective in helping others to help themselves to change.

There are more examples of how the ego causes many of the other specific behaviours at the back of the book.

The Real Meaning of Transformation

Much has been said and written about the process of self-transformation. But only the ego makes it necessary. If you break the word 'transformation' down, you will find three words or three ideas within the concept of transformation. *Trans* means transcend or rise above. *Form* which means form or shape. *Ation* means action. Ego means the self has trapped itself in an image that is created by the self within the self (consciousness) on the screen of the mind. As the self identifies itself with the image, it's as if the self gives itself the 'form' of that image, and all thoughts and feelings are shaped by that false image of the self. And as we have seen these thoughts, emotions and behaviours constitute suffering … always. Trans**form**ation of the self takes place when the self **transcends** the image to which it has become attached i.e. detaches from the image on the screen of the mind, thereby 'shaking off' the **form** of the image, so that the self is no longer shaped by the image.

This completely changes the thought/emotion/action sequence within the self. So if you want to transform your thinking and therefore your life there is no need to struggle with your thoughts and feelings, no need to change or develop your personality. All you have to do is detach, let go of the image that you are attached to, and identifying with, in your own mind. Everything flows from there. In other words, correct your sense of identity. Stop identifying with what you are not.

In truth, there is no such thing as 'self' transformation simply because the self can never be anything other than its 'self'. Illusion arises when the self 'believes' its self to be something other than it's self. The self has trapped its self in a belief. Realising this and rising above, and therefore 'out of' what you believe your self to be, and simply 'being your self' again, is transformation.

The Art of Non-Attachment

In summary, ego is almost the same as attachment. If attachment is the root cause of our emotional suffering then learning not to attach seems the obvious solution and way to a pain-free life. And it is. But it's not an instant solution, simply because the habit of attaching (misidentifying) is so subtle that it takes a little time to clearly see and break the habit.

This is where the practice of meditation is essential in 'noticing' when and to what you attach your self. Meditation is not a goal in itself. If you make it a goal, you'll be disappointed and waste much time. Meditation is the cultivation of self-awareness, it is a process of 'seeing' and a way of being. In your meditation you will clearly see that 'you' don't actually get attached to an external object. You will see that you are attaching to the image of the object, and that image is created by you on the screen of your mind. Detachment means learning to create the image of the object but not losing your sense of self in the image of the object.

The first step of meditation is often referred to as 'detached observation'. In meditation you are learning to just observe what is passing across the screen of your mind. To begin with, it is not a question of trying to control your thoughts, simply watching, observing, witnessing, what arises on the screen of your mind. After some practice you will be able to do this with greater ease wherever you and whenever you need to e.g. in the meeting when other egos are clashing, in the car, in the kitchen, at your desk, in conversations with others.

As you practice your meditation, which really means as you become more self-aware (not self-consciousness or self-obsessed), you will also begin to see why you feel what you feel, why certain emotions keep appearing, why certain reactions are almost guaranteed to erupt in the same situations with the same people.

And when you see that the root cause of these 'reactions' is always attachment and therefore misidentification, it becomes much easier to let go and allow your behaviour to change naturally, as it will. You won't need to struggle to change a behaviour, or even a feeling. Simply see and let go. Everything flows from there.

So why do you attempt to attach your self to anything in the first place? It's simply one of those learned beliefs that says if you can acquire and hold on to 'things', even if it/they not tangible, then it/they will either:

- ~ Complete you
- ~ Make you feel better (happier)
- ~ Give you more power over others
- ~ Signify your life is a success
- ~ Prove you are a winner
- ~ Help you to survive
- ~ Enhance your self-worth/esteem

But these are false beliefs to which we/you/I all become attached, to some extent or other. They are illusions that keep us trapped in a lifetime of grasping and attaching, and therefore suffering.

Home Truths

To free your self from attaching to and identifying with something 'you' are not i.e. to liberate your self from ego, there are seven 'home truths' that only you can prove to your self:

1. **Complete you**

   You don't need to add anything to your self to be complete in your self. *In truth*, you cannot add anything to your self. You can add things to your body, but not to your self.

2. **Make you feel better (happier)**

   You don't have to acquire anything to make you feel better. *In truth* you need to let go of everything to be free, and only when you are free can you feel happy, which really means contented.

3. **Give you more power over others**

   You can never have power/control over others because every human being regardless of size, age, background is a unique stand-alone 'power unit'. *In truth,* you can only have power (control) over your own mental, intellectual and physical faculties.

4. **Signify your life is a success**

   Success in life is not acquisition, it's not about who gets the most toys wins. *In truth,* success has more to do with your ability to be content in any situation and respond calmly and positively when all around are in a state of panic and fear. That requires all your power – power that will not be available when you are attached to something or someone.

5. **Prove you are a winner**

   Winners in life are not 'go-getters' as so many of us have been schooled.

The real winners are the 'go-givers' because that's what wins the respect and trust of others. *In truth*, we are designed to give, to contribute, to share, to radiate and, when you do, life rushes to your door.

6. **Help you to survive**

   When you realize that you are not the form that you occupy, when you realize you are simply consciousness, simply spirit/soul/self and not your body, then survival ceases to be an issue because you will also know that you cannot not survive...so to speak. *In truth*, only the body dies and becomes food. You don't!

7. **Enhance your self worth/esteem**

   You probably already know that it is a fatal mistake to base your self-worth on any 'thing/s' outside your self, because at any moment the universe can, and will, come and take those things away. And you know you have absolutely no control. Which is why most people live a life of perpetual insecurity.

In truth your worth is infinite and unlimited because 'you' the 'I' that says 'I am', is infinite and unlimited. But to see and know that to be true, will require that you release all that you are attached to, because it's all finite and limited. Hence the value of the practice of daily meditation.

It is impossible to add anything to your self. The illusion that you can add something to you stems from the moment you were taught to believe you were a body, a physical form. You can add more clothes to your body, more stuff to your home, more trophies to your cabinet, but you can add nothing to your self. If you can see this, know this and live this, you are almost home. If you understand this, realize this here and now, in this moment, then you don't need to do any more, or even read any further. All you have to do is watch when you fall back into the old illusions above, have a little chuckle to your self and drop them again. Observing, watching, seeing, letting go are all included in the art of meditation. Which is why meditation is not just something that you do sitting quietly in a corner (although such moments of practice are necessary). Meditation is the cultivation of self awareness wherever you are. And just as plants will grow gradually when they are cultivated and nurtured, so too your self-awareness will grow when you nurture your meditation practice.

To practice meditation:

Sit quietly
Relax your body and rest your gaze on a point in front of you
Gently concentrate your attention on your self
Become aware of your self
Let any thoughts and feelings come and go
Be aware of your self being aware of your self
Notice a peacefulness arising from within your being
Allow that peace to fill your being
Know your self as peace
Be at peace

Tap Tap Tap!

One of the most recent methods to free yourself from a lifetime of accumulated and stored emotions is to tap certain parts of your body, a set number of times, in certain places, in a set sequence. By all accounts, it works as a way of releasing the emotional energy of the past that has been trapped and stored in the physical structures and cells of your body. The releasing of that trapped energy then has a subtle effect on your mind without you being fully aware of it. Tapping helps to clear your emotional records. However, it only deals with the emotional energy already created and stored. It does little to alter the cause of the creation of that emotional energy, which is always attachment. Only with detachment from the ideas, images, beliefs and concepts that we habitually cling to within our consciousness is it then possible to 'tap in' to the deeper truths and wisdom at the heart of our consciousness. Only then do we deal with 'cause' of the emotion and not just the symptoms.

The Seven Strategies of Detachment

After a lifetime of 'attaching', developing the art of non-attachment will not happen overnight. In the meantime here are some ways to practice detachment in daily life until you reach the point when you don't need a method.

Strategy 1
Change your relationship from possessor to trustee
Use this when you become too attached to your possessions. Remind yourself, nothing actually belongs to you. You cannot, in reality, own anything . However, you are a 'trustee' of every 'thing' that comes into your life until the time comes for someone else to have it in their life! Seeing your self as a trustee in your relationships with objects and positions loosens the attachment and diminishes the fear of loss, until you fully realize that nothing is MINE! Or in the well worn words of that old saying, "You can't take *it* with you when you go". So it makes sense to stop trying to hold on to *it* while it's here. *Use this* until you fully realize you cannot possess or own anything or anyone.

Strategy 2
Let go
Use this when you are holding on to a specific opinion/point of view. Next time you find yourself in an argument, disarm the other by simply saying,

"I don't agree with you but I accept that is your point of view. Tell me more, so that I may understand why you see it that way." *Use this* until you fully realize you can never be more right than anyone else and you can never 'make' anyone else see your rightness. And keep using this until you realize there is no right and wrong in the universe of consciousness.

Strategy 3
Practice giving

Use this when you recognise yourself to be frequently if not always wanting/desiring something from others. When you want something, you are already attached to the object of your desire. Where? On the screen of your mind. Almost all of us learn this habit from the moment we are born. It sounds like, "Gimme gimme gimme!" Break this habit by consciously practicing ways of giving that are free of any desire for anything in return. *Use this* until you realize that you create your life through giving and not taking, until you fully see that to give (to others) is to receive (from your self).

Strategy 4
Mentally rehearse different outcomes

Use this when you are fearful of change, which means you are attached to, and too comfortable with, the way things are, or when you are holding on to some form of self-limitation (I can't). All the top performers in most sports now realize and use the power that comes from mental rehearsal or visualisation. Take a few minutes to visualise future changes, as a preparation to embrace those changes when they arrive in actuality. See yourself doing what you previously thought you couldn't. *Use this* until you realize that the only thing that never changes in life is the 'I' that observes everything else changing, and you are that 'I'!

Strategy 5
Don't identify with the situation/outcome

Use this in any process, anytime and anywhere in life. This simply means don't make your happiness dependent on something outside your self, especially the result of yours or others' actions. Be content, whatever the outcome of anything. That does not mean things cannot be improved, it just means the journey is as important as the destination. Enjoy the journey. Happiness, which really means contentment, is a choice and a decision, not a random experience or a dependency. Do good, and in the doing of the good, you will notice your happiness arising naturally. *Use this* until you fully realize everything that is happening at any moment, close and far, is exactly what is meant to be happening at that moment.

Strategy 6
Imagine someone else dealing with the situation – how would they deal with it?
Use this when your attachment is obviously sabotaging your ability to interact calmly with others. Take a moment to imagine how someone, whose wisdom you respect, would handle the situation. This loosens your grip on your way or 'my perception', and will ultimately weaken your habits of reaction. If they are nearby, sit with them and ask them how they would respond. *Use this* until you develop the power and the wisdom to deal calmly and positively with whatever arises in life.

Strategy 7
Look at the situation through the eyes of the other party
Appropriate in all conflict situations – this forces you to release your attachment to your point of view, from your position, and to generate an understanding of the other's perception and position. Ask, listen, ask, listen, ask, listen, is the secret to understanding the others point of view. As you do you will see though the eyes of the other and free yourself in the process. *Use this* until you fully realize you cannot control others but you can influence others and that's all you can do. *Use this* until you are able to fully free your self from wanting anything from anyone!

Only when you are the master of detachment, or non-attachment, will you be able to free yourself from your emotional reactions, as all emotions have their roots in attachment and therefore the ego. At this point the most frequent question is, "But isn't human emotion both natural and healthy?"

That depends entirely on what you mean by emotion. And that depends entirely on the level of your emotional intelligence or your ability to recognise and identify the emotions that you feel.

So let's cultivate our EQ a little and, in the process, liberate our self from more of those myths that currently run the world.

The Emotional Rollercoaster

Twenty years ago, the term Emotional Intelligence was almost unheard off. During the last decade or so, the subject of Emotional Intelligence has spawned many books, seminars, workshops and 'heated' conversations! It's been a hot topic in the universe of training and development and has even entered the corporate world. Only in the past few years has some form of learning around emotions entered mainstream education following a growing recognition of a significant deficiency in children's capacity to master their own feelings and form healthy relationships.

However, it seems there is still a huge confusion around the true nature of emotion and what it means to feel. This is because the ego is not fully understood. It is not yet widely recognized that the ego is the root of all emotion. That's not to say all emotions are bad, or that you shouldn't get emotional. It just means that like the ego, emotion is a mistake. More accurately it is the result of 'the' mistake.

So let's proceed to the very heart of our emotions where we may just discover that emotions have no heart, where we may realize that emotions do not come from the heart, where it may be seen that all emotion is suffering and all suffering has an emotional component, where we may at long last unravel the precise difference between emotions and feelings and begin to learn both **how** to feel and **what** to feel … again!

Emotional Intelligence or Emotional Confusion?

Throughout the world, every Saturday afternoon, hundreds of thousands of fully grown mature males of the human species will make their weekly pilgrimage to their temples of worship throughout the land. It is there that some of them will display more emotion in 90 minutes than they did during the previous six days. When the other team scores, they will descend into misery and perhaps despair. And when their team scores they will jump up and down with glee and what is commonly mistaken for happiness, namely excitement. For one and half hours, and perhaps many hours afterwards, their emotions will be in the hands of 22 men in shorts kicking a ball up and down a piece of grass.

So what are they attached to? Their team. Not just attached, they have completely identified themselves with the team. And what's wrong with that you may say? Well nothing is wrong as such, in the sense that nothing is wrong! In the grand scheme of things, all is as it should be. But it is a classic example of misidentification. You are not a football team. You are you. But if you identify with the team, it means you surrender control over what you feel to eleven men kicking a ball.

Over time, this will become exhausting, weakening, disempowering. And very unhealthy. But if you suggest this to a football fan be prepared to receive much resistance. You will be seen as a threat to their drug of choice, as emotion in itself is just another addiction. Just as drugs can induce highs and lows in our moods, so our attachments induce highs and lows called emotions. And just as drugs become addictive so our attachments and the emotions they induce become addictive.

Sometimes you see the neutral spectator watching the same game. They don't identify with either side, but they applaud the excellence of all the skills on view. They appreciate the whole game. They don't become 'excited' or 'sad' when either team scores. They don't become dependent on the events in front of them to stimulate their emotional state. They don't 'take from' the scene of the match as much as 'give to' what they are watching. And what they give is appreciation. This is not tiring, not weakening, not disempowering, because they are empowering others with that appreciation. And as they do, they empower themselves. But to the die-hard fan, committed and attached to their team, that just sounds silly. They would say, "Where's the enjoyment in that?" What they mean is, "Where's the excitement in that?" Which means they are addicted not only to their team but also to the visual stimulation of watching their team. And 'where is' what they are watching? It seems to be on the pitch out there but in reality they are watching the game on the screen of their mind, that's where the 'attachment' is happening. In the meantime, what are the ladies doing? Well some are also at the game. But many others are 'in store' doing their 'shawpping', creating some new attachments of their own!

So we have arrived in that wonderfully internal, invisible and intangible territory, of which more has probably been written in the last 15 years than in the last 150 years. It is the inner terrain of our emotions and our feelings. This is where things become very 'interesting' and somewhat revealing. Let me ask you to either close the book for moment, or go to a blank page/space at the back, and write down your definition of **emotion** and your definition of **feeling**. It is an essential exercise if you are to take your self beyond the beliefs that you may have assimilated about emotions/feelings, and to see and know the truth for your self.

As you challenge your self and reflect on what these inner phenomena are, recall and re-experience some emotion from a past event, and then look into it to see why the emotion arose, where it arose from, and the exact nature of the emotion etc. Take a moment to do that now. Define 'emotion' and 'feeling', then come back to this page.

As you probably noticed, it's not easy to get a clear sense of what emotion is and what feeling is, even when you sit and consciously look within. Whenever I ask this question in seminars probably less than 3% of people get anywhere near a clear definition of emotion in which they are confident. Even fewer have a clear awareness of the difference between the two, often confusing one with the other. Some say emotions are internal and feelings are external, while others say the other way round. Some say you can't control emotions but you can control feelings. Some say emotions are feelings and feelings are emotions. Others say emotion is a reaction whereas feeling is what happens after the reaction.

What makes this all the more interesting is that if you stand back for a moment and consider your whole 'life' in general, what do you see but a series of relationships. Life is essentially relationship. And what will be the most frequent currency of exchange in all our relationships? Our emotions and our feelings. And yet we don't even know what they are. So much for our education. Did someone decide we shouldn't know? Unlikely, but many have since realized the advantages that can be gained by invoking human emotions on a massive scale. They are commonly known as advertising and marketing executives!

If you ever find yourself in a conversation about emotions, trying to understand where they come form, whether they are good or bad, you will make absolutely no progress unless you start with a clear and agreed definition and description of how they are created. In fact, if you don't first agree a definition and a cause of emotion, the conversation is likely to go nowhere fast and become somewhat... emotional!

So let me share with you a definition of *emotion* (we'll come to feeling a little later). Once again, like the definition of ego, it's not carved in stone, but it's the one I would like to work with here. If it doesn't work for you then you can throw it out and construct your own after you finish the book. So let me invite you to work with this definition and description and 'see' how true or accurate it is in your experience.

Emotion is...

**...the disturbance of the energy of your consciousness
when the object of attachment is
damaged, threatened, moved or lost**

Are you a perfectionist? Have you ever watched a perfectionist? The perfectionist walks into the room and walks up to a cabinet shelf in the corner and promptly moves the vase two inches to the left, while saying with much irritation, "Who moved that vase, it should be THERE and it should be turned to face outwards exactly like THIS!"

In other words, when things are not exactly perfect, the perfectionist creates a disturbance in their consciousness which is called emotion because someone moved the object of attachment. In other words, the perfectionist has created an image of the vase on the screen of their mind and they identify with that image so that when the world 'out there', in this case the vase on the shelf, does not fit exactly the image in their mind to which they are 'attached', they take it personally and thereby create an emotional disturbance called irritation in their own consciousness. Phew! Fortunately the disturbance passes quite fast and normal service is resumed, until the next imperfection is spotted! Are you familiar with this?

If we return to the scratched car for a moment. There is a disturbance in the energy of your consciousness because someone has *damaged* the object of attachment. You are the creator of the disturbance called anger, not Mr Scratcher. Have you ever lost your car keys. Notice that the longer it takes to find them the more intense the emotion of anxiety becomes. Why? Because you have *lost* an object that you are attached to and dependent upon. The disturbance which you create in your consciousness is called anxiety. The moment you find your car keys, notice how, with a big sigh of relief, all the anxiety melts away.

The dictionary definition of emotion is much simpler. Emotion is defined as...

Agitation of mind.

I've simply expanded one official description to include the mechanism by which the E of C becomes M. In other words how the Energy of Consciousness (self) becomes Motion. Or E Motion... Energy in Motion.

Perhaps you are now thinking, as many people do at this point, that what is implied here is that all emotion is negative. I prefer not to use the terms negative or positive as it's too black and white. In the territory of consciousness, nothing is black and white. But yes, if you are thinking that, then you are going in the right direction, because what I am saying is that ALL emotion is unhealthy. It is a signal that you are not in alignment with the true you, the egoless you, the authentic you. Simply because all emotion, as it's defined here, is the result of the ego (attachment)...always. And ego, as we have seen, is the deepest 'unhealthiness' that we can create and know. But still, it's just a mistake, and mistakes can be corrected.

Hunting for Love and Happiness

This brings us to the question that naturally follows - isn't LOVE an emotion? Isn't HAPPINESS an emotion? And when asked, most people tend to nod their heads in the affirmative with a, "Yes of course they are." That's what many of us have been taught and what we pass on. But after more than 25 years of research, much meditative contemplation, and many deep and meaningful conversations, it has become obvious that this is where one of the greatest, all-pervasive confusions in life begins. What you could call the origins of 'emotional confusion'. It is at this inner frontier of our emotions and feelings that definitions are twisted, descriptions are distorted, and meaning is lost.

If you spend enough time exploring the true meaning of love and happiness you will realize that they are two of the most misused and abused words in our language. When we use the word LOVE, we usually 'mean' something else such as *Desire, Attachment, Dependency or Identification*.

What LOVE is NOT

These four primary confusions about love are assimilated at an early age. They are innocently passed down from generation to generation, strengthened and magnified by Hollywood in particular, and marketing in general. They are built into our language and our culture and yet they only serve to sustain the creation of stress within ourselves and conflict within our relationships.

1 Love is mistaken for DESIRE
When you go to the movies and watch the classic love story there is usually a moment when he says to her, "Darling, I love you." But what he really means is, "I want you. I want to be with you. I want you to be mine... tonight!". And of course she reciprocates with an, "I love you too." Which often means, "I've got you!" But true love doesn't desire or possess. True love doesn't want anything. As we saw earlier love is already complete and its only intention is to connect and to give, not acquire.

2 Love is mistaken for ATTACHMENT
When we say, "I love my football team or I love my new car or I love my garden." It's not love. Once again it's a misuse of the word love. What we really 'mean' is, "I am attached to my football team, I am attached to my new car". And love is not attachment, if for no other reason than all attachment causes fear, and fear in this dualistic world is the opposite of love. Fear is love distorted by attachment.

3 Love is mistaken for DEPENDENCY
When we say, "I love my cocaine. I love my morning coffee. I love going to the gym"… this is to confuse love with dependency. Love is not dependent on anything. We are really saying we believe these things make us happy. They seem to, but it's not authentic happiness, as we shall see.

4 Love is mistaken for IDENTIFICATION
More commonly some say, "I love my nation, I love my country." Again, this is not love, it's identification. We are identifying with a national identity, which in itself is a mistake. 'I am' is not a nationality. Love does not identify with anything that is not itself. We have already seen that as soon as it does, ego takes birth and therefore suffering (emotion) arises.

What HAPPINESS is NOT
Similarly we misuse the word happiness. When we use the word happy what we more often really mean is *Acquisition, Stimulation, Consumption or Relief.* These mistakes in meaning, which are simply careless uses of the word happiness, have become embedded in the language of our consumer society which is the language of advertising.

1 Happiness is mistaken for ACQUISITION

When we say something like, "The new carpet has just arrived, I am so happy," this is not real happiness, it's an acquisition of an external object called a carpet, in which we quickly lose our identity. And then it's not long before we may hear or shout, "Aargh! who stained my new carpet!" And as we saw, in that moment it's as if you are saying, "I am a carpet!" Not a happy moment.

2 Happiness is mistaken for STIMULATION

Coming out of the cinema, we can be heard to say something like, "Wow, wasn't that just a great movie, it made me feel so happy". But it's not true happiness, because the self is dependent on a source of stimulation which can never be sustained. It is a 'stimulated experience', which, like all other stimulations, if mistaken for happiness, will lead to dependency and addiction and a great deal of unhappiness.

3 Happiness is mistaken for CONSUMPTION

We all know that moment when we say, "This is my favourite ice cream, or favourite chocolate, I am so happy." OK maybe we don't say, "I am so happy," but it's what we mean. Again this is not real happiness as the feeling is dependent on sensual stimulation that also cannot be sustained. All stimulation is excitation and excitation is not happiness, it's excitation.

4 Happiness is mistaken for RELIEF

Returning from the dentist, we might be heard to hoot with a little joy, "The toothache has gone, I am so happy." Once again it's not true happiness, it's relief from pain. And relief from pain is not happiness, it's relief.

So WHAT IS Love and Happiness?

How do we know that in all the examples above we are misusing the words love and happiness? They are all forms of *dependency*. They are all dependent on something external to the self. And authentic love and happiness are not dependent on anything. As we intuitively know true love is unconditional and therefore not dependent on anything outside the self.

So what is love? Earlier we explored some of the common myths about love and began to explore the true nature of love as the invisible and intangible energy that both radiates outwards from the heart of every human being. It is what connects, unites and holds us all together. Here is another way to describe and define love that is a little more active.

LOVE is…the natural expression of our self, or the giving of our self, in the form of

> **sharing**
> **helping**
> **encouraging**
> **empowering**
> **accepting**
> **appreciating**
> **celebrating…**
> **(and many other 'expressions')**

….without wanting anything in return and with the intention of benefiting the other.

As soon as you want something back, it's not love, it's business. As soon as you seek something in return you start doing subtle deals that may eventually compromise and perhaps sabotage the relationship. This is why expectation is often the seed of the downfall of many relationships. Love has no expectations upon which personal happiness is dependent, only a positive vision for 'the other' and their endeavors.

We all know what we feel when we don't get what we want. Yet love's intention is always to ensure the other's needs are met first. And from the highest point of view, which many describe as the spiritual point of view, the greatest need of almost everyone today is to realize love is what you are, it is what 'I am', not what you need. If there is a need it is the need to realize there is nothing that you need! Only then can you be fully free, without an agenda in your relationships. Only then can you give of your self without feeling as if you are draining your self.

Only then can you be fully present for the other. If you are not present then love is not present.

HAPPINESS on the other hand is…
…the contentment of the self when I know my own true wealth within, and want nothing from others - authentic happiness is not conditional or dependent on any other person, any event or circumstance.

Happiness arises naturally from within when the self is free of needing and desiring, when the self stops attempting to acquire and accumulate and has realized 'I am' all I can ever be and nothing is missing. It arises naturally when your energy, which is you, is given without condition. Only when all craving and dependency are gone, only when you end grasping and attaching, can you be contentedly happy. In essence: peace is…truth guides …love does…happiness rewards.

Yes there is a kind of happiness when you get the new toy, receive the gift, see your team win, eat you favourite food etc. but it is of the transient and dependent type. What must follow this stimulated high is the low. Some say that the highs and lows are part of life's rich pageant. It's true, they are, it's just that over time the highs get harder to hit and therefore lower, and the lows become deeper and harder to get out of. And as any addict will confirm, you need progressively more drug to reach any high at all, until one day it's all low. That's why any 'emotional high' is not authentic happiness, just stimulation.

Sensation Seekers

When we fall into the trap of making our source of love and happiness external, material, physical things, we start to become dependent on the sensations they produce. We become sensation seekers. It all stems from the first 'misidentification', the first attachment, the first dependency, which is to our physical bodies. Our sense of identity becomes physical. That identity then extends to all the labels we give to our body (size, gender, features). Then to all the labels we give to things we relate to through our body (position, pay, possessions) Then it seems that the only way to 'feel' these 'stimulations', which we confuse with love and happiness, is through our physical senses. Love and happiness are then mistakenly seen as only possible through physical sensation and stimulation.

The solution is not new. It's not even old. It's ancient. It's called self-realization, which means realising one's true identity and one's true nature. To know ones self and ones nature is to know the self as the place of peace, as a source of love and as a space from which happiness arises in your own life. Hence the saying 'the seeker is the sought'. There are two ways you can arrive at the awareness of who and what you really are and therefore restore your connection to your heart, where true love and authentic happiness are in permanent residence.

The Realization of Self

The first route to the realisation of the 'I' that says 'I AM' is the scientific route. Just as science creates a theory and then conducts experiments to affirm the truth or the reality of the theory, so the self contemplates a theory of WHO I AM. The laboratory is consciousness, the method is meditation, the raw materials are thoughts, the measures of progress are feelings, insight and awareness, and the result of the internal experiment is 'self realization'. First the theory, which is not new, and goes something like this.

The 'I' is a conscious 'being' that is self aware. Consciousness is energy but not an energy that you can see with physical eyes. This energy is indestructible and is often referred to as spirit, soul or the authentic self. It is not separate from the self. It is the ME that says 'I AM ME!' It is the life force that animates the form. It is 'I'. And the original and unchanging nature of the 'I' is peaceful and loving.

That's the theory in words and ideas. The experiment is then conducted in the laboratory of consciousness and its aim, like all scientific experiments, is to validate or invalidate the theory. The methodology is meditation. As the self meditates upon the ideas/beliefs/concepts contained within the theory, it focuses its entire attention inwards upon such thoughts. Gradually, as those thoughts (above) become deeper, they penetrate the heart of consciousness while at the same time fading into silence. It's as if they knock on the door of the heart and, as the heart of the self opens, there is insight (sight in) into the heart, into the self, and the 'realisation' of 'I am' and that nothing need be added to 'I am'. There is not even the thought 'I am', simply pure awareness. In that moment, the self 'insperiences' the highest reality, and it is silent and still, yet radiantly peaceful. The self realizes the self as pure awareness.

From that moment, all other 'learned identities' have no power over the self, which is now in its original and true state, and they dissolve into the background (well almost) as they are clearly seen to be 'the illusions of 'I' that they are.

Remembering 'I AM"

The maintenance of self realization, or the realized self, then becomes the inner work of day-to-day life. The insight (sight in) into who I am is sustained by 're-memorisation'. The lifetime habit of identifying with what you are not is so strong that there are inevitable moments through the day when you fall asleep to your true self awareness, and back into misidentification. There is a requirement to make an 'effort' to remember, remind and restore your consciousness, your self, as the 'I' that says I AM, as pure awareness, and nothing more.

This memorization and re-memorization over time weakens the habit of allowing old false identities to re-invade your consciousness and thereby hijack your thoughts and feelings. As the self stabilizes its self in pure self awareness, your true sense of your own pure being becomes clear and consistent. This is the road to being egoless, often referred to as the 'liberation of the soul'. In one sense you are already there because you cannot be anything but your self. However it's those habits of misidentification that require attention and awareness, the practice of 'seeing though' them, and the letting go.

One sure sign that self-realization is genuine is a change of perception. There is a perceptual shift from seeing others as the enemy and therefore as potential threats, from seeing the world as a place of struggle and survival and therefore dangerous, to where you are able to accept and embrace everyone, because you now see them also a beings of pure awareness (even when they may not see themselves that way), and you see the world as an opportunity to embrace and dance with all of life… metaphorically speaking.

Process of Elimination

The second route back to being your authentic self is the process of elimination. This is similar to stripping off your many layers of clothing to reveal your naked physical form. By seeing what you are not, what the 'I' is not, you gradually 'uncloak' the true self who is always present and naked at the center. Instead of starting with WHO AM I, experiment with WHO or WHAT AM I NOT?

Then identify all the things that you identify with in the revealing light of your awareness, challenge each with the question IS THAT WHAT I AM? It will not be long before you start to see what you are not. That will include those 'things' that we explored earlier, like your nationality, your profession, your location, even your family etc. They are all either labels or ideas or concepts. They are the 'things' that are not 'I'. As you proceed, you may catch a glimpse of the truth that you are also not your race, gender and even your body, as they are not what the 'I' that says 'I am'…is. Once again they are labels or, in the case of the body, just the piece of meat and bone that is animated by the 'I'.

If you stick with it, at an even subtler level, you also will begin to see and eliminate all the things you momentarily believe are you, but are not. Things like your thoughts, feelings and even your beliefs and memories can also be a source of a false sense of identity. It becomes obvious that all of these subtler 'things', like all other 'things', come and go, and yet the 'I', the ME, always remains.

So what is left after the process of elimination, after peeling away all the layers of false identity, all your false pretences? Nothing is left. No thing. Only awareness. This can sound a bit scary in theory. It can sound like a complete loss of identity. In reality however, it is the restoration of 'true identity' because identity was already regularly and habitually lost in all those other 'things'. In truth, your real identity is no identity. At least not an identity that can be 'captured' in words, ideas or concepts. They can only 'point' towards what you are. This restoration of a pure 'I am' awareness is not an idea or a theory, that would be to identify again with just another idea or theory. Identity is beyond theories, concepts and ideas. And so...at the end of the process of elimination, you are left with an awareness of your self as awareness, as the one who is aware of being aware. While this sounds abstract (as it must in physical language), in practice and in reality (of consciousness), it is both freeing and energising.

Time to Play Again

What falls away is all the fighting and defending of what were false identities, all the struggling and striving to survive the perceived threats to those identities, and all the emotional suffering and the stress that have their roots in attempting to build and maintain those false identities. You no longer have to keep up any false pretence. You no longer have to pretend to be something you are not. If you want to keep pretending that's also fine. But now, like the actor on the stage, you are aware that you are pretending and it's an opportunity to create high quality pretending, which is fun, because you infuse your creativity with love and through your playfulness you bring that love to others.

While you may occasionally 'appear' to be really serious, or seriously real, behind your apparent seriousness, you take nothing seriously, as you know it's just a game. So you play the game. A game called life. And when you do see another suffering within the game of life you play the role of 'being there for them' as you extend your self, your love, from one being to another being, knowing that their suffering is rooted in their taking it all to seriously. You know that they have not yet realised that they suffer because they believe they are someone/something that they are not. They have forgotten and not yet re-realised it's a game, a play, an opportunity to 'play creatively', joyfully, with others. Being playful is to allow the purpose life to find its way back into this world. A playful being is love in action, it is loves dance on Earth.

Just Being

Freeing your 'self' from all that you have trapped your 'self' within, releases a long suppressed enthusiasm for life and the joy of living. However until there is this revealing of the self to the self so to speak, many will resist and fight against this idea of being 'no thing' and say things like, "But I like to struggle... I need to fight...life and suffering go together...don't they.. isn't that part of being someone?" They are really saying they are a little addicted to the emotional pain of living, a pain they have not yet realized they create themselves, or that is not yet so intense they have to do something about it. For them, the question, WHO AM I, is irrelevant...at the moment!

Only by eliminating all the things you are not will you reveal what's left which is you. And what's left? The pure awareness of the 'I' that says I am. Nothing more. Just...I am. No thoughts. Not even the thought 'I am'. Just pure awareness. You can't see it, touch it, smell it, burn it, cut it, drown it. Yet the awareness of 'I' is more real than anything you have ever known. It is to be, and know, yourself as you truly are.

Yes of course you still have to make breakfast, go to the office, buy Christmas presents for the kids. You may even still watch the movie or the match. But the difference is you no longer take it seriously. You care, but you don't become serious, because your happiness is no longer dependent on any person, any event, any result or any object. You are a free spirit... again. In your freedom, happiness as 'contentment' is your nature. You need no reason to be happy, you just are contented. Love is your natural intention and you need no special occasion to be loving, you just are. And the unshakable platform upon which they (love and contentment) stand is the power of your peace. No thing, no one, no event, can ever surprise you, shock you or shake you. Ever again. You cannot strive to be this. It's not work, it's not a job to be done. You arrive back at this, your natural state of being, through a process of 'seeing' and realising. The only effort is in watching, and as you watch, becoming aware that you are the watcher. Then you 'see' what is not you. You see through the illusions that you have been creating about your self and about others. All that is transient and temporary is not you. It's real, but a lot less real than the reality of you.

Developing Your Practice

Being 'here', being centred and watching the circling activity of life moving, changing, rising, falling, ebbing and flowing around your self, without attaching and identifying, without getting 'sucked in', requires practice. However it's only when you actually start to practice that the gap between theory and practice becomes apparent. As always theory is easy and practice...challenging.

So here, in as few words as possible, is the practice:

Sit in a quiet space
Watch attentively
Withdraw inwardly
Watch even more attentively
But without tension
Notice who is watching
See all that is being watched is moving
But notice the watcher is still
Everything watched passes
Only the watcher remains
And there YOU are
The Watcher
Watching
Beyond time
Beyond space
Just watching
Fully present
Here
Now
Watching

As you practice remember to expect nothing, compare not with others, and never attempt to repeat whatever 'insperience' you may have.

Emotional Confusion, Illusion and Delusion

I was going to say 'most' of us are 'emotionally confused' but it's probably more accurate to say ALL of us are, because we have all caught the same form of a spiritual virus we now know as EGO. All emotion comes from the ego but we are not aware of it. We are not even aware that we are emotionally confused. Without cultivating self awareness, it's not easy to discern the difference between certain emotions, never mind see how we create them.

This lack of emotional awareness results in an inability to recognise the emotions that we feel, dissolve those emotions and not create them in the first place. When we do try to control or dissolve the emotions that we create we usually make a hash of it and just make them even more powerful. All this lies at the heart of what has been called Emotional Intelligence this past decade. It seems very few notice that the more emotional you become the less intelligent you can be, especially around the subject of ...emotions.

So before we explore the specific emotional confusions that tend to rule all our lives it's worth understanding the idea of intelligence. What is intelligence? A simple definition goes something like this:

Intelligence is using what you KNOW, in the right way, in the right place, at the right moment and with the right intention.

If you don't 'know', and you know that you don't know, then the intelligent thing to do is to admit that you don't know. While some know what they don't know, many others just don't know what they don't know. Which is 'pure' ignorance. If they act out of that ignorance it is unlikely they will do the right thing in the right way at the right moment.

For the purpose of our exploration into love, you could say the 'intelligence of the self' lies in three domains – the rational, emotional and spiritual, to which a fourth can be added, namely 'intuitive intelligence'.

Rational Intelligence (IQ)

This is what we develop in the school classroom, as well as the school of life. It is essentially the use of information, experience, thought and reason to arrive at a decision in a rational way. It's a bit slow and requires much thinking through. We will often say "I just need to think about this". It's noisy in the mind and it can be tiring. It's the logical but slow way to make decisions. For example, at an early stage in life, you receive the information that, if you step out onto the road when cars are coming, and if your body collides with one of those cars, it will result in a lot of pain and perhaps the death of your body. The rationally intelligent use of that information is to cross the road when there are no cars to knock your body over, or at least to walk in between the cars as they pass. You are intelligently using what you know about bodies and cars, in the right way, in the right place, at the right time with the intention of staying alive and unhurt. Those who do not know about what happens when bodies hit cars, or those who forget, would be said to be ignorant of the relationship between cars, speed and human bodies, and therefore unintelligent, as they walk out in front of the traffic. So far so obvious.

Intuitive Intelligence

Intuition tends to be perceived as an exclusively feminine trait but it's something we all have but seldom consciously develop. Intuition is when a certain 'knowingness' arises within your consciousness, for which there is no rational explanation. More a feeling than a thought. Someone may say, "Why are you going this way and not that way," and you say, "I don't know why, it just 'feels' right." You make a decision based on an immediate feeling, as opposed to at the end of a logical thought process. While thinking something through takes time and creates much mental noise, feeling is an instant 'seeing' with your inner eye. This eye is sometimes referred to as 'intellect'. Not intellect in an academic sense, but intellect as in your ability to see and 'discern' the quality of an idea, or how aligned to the truth an insight may be. Intellect is the second faculty of our consciousness and it can operate *rationally* or *intuitively*.

When your intellect is operating intuitively, decisions take almost no time and little energy. Intuition bubbles to the surface of your consciousness and into the light of your awareness, from the silent heart of your being.

At the heart of each one of us is an innate wisdom. Intuition is our ability to hear that wisdom so that you can discern what is true and what is out of alignment with the truth. It is the quiet voice of our 'inner tutor' that is always available to guide us. It is speaking to us at all times, but we more often fail to hear it as we are habitually busy creating mental noise of thinking. Ask most scientists, entrepreneurs, business people and inventors, and many will tell you that their best decisions and most powerful insights were more often intuitive. Usually in the bath or in some similarly relaxed setting. The practice of meditation is the great facilitator of intuition, as you learn to quieten the mind and then feel and hear the subtle voice of your inner tutor, the wisdom of your own heart.

Spiritual Intelligence (SQ)

There is something innately beautiful about spiritual intelligence if only because all that is ugly within our consciousness must be gone before this intelligence can flower within the self. That ugliness is of course the ego, the habit of attachment that we explored earlier. While the self is spirit (often called soul or the authentic self), spiritual intelligence is only possible when the self is not attached to any ideas or concepts of the self, including the 'idea' that I am spirit/soul! Pure self awareness is not based on the thought 'I am awareness'. Thought is quiet. The self just is, and it is in that 'isness', this 'I am'ness, that beauty is seen and known. That beauty is truth. The truth is that which never changes, that which is eternal. The 'insperience' of ones own eternity is the first aspect of the truth of onself that is realised. The eternal beauty of the self as peace, as love, as joy, is also seen and known, not as ideas or concepts as they appear here, but in their reality as the self. It is from this state of being, this awareness of truth, that the ability to be, to know and to do the right thing, in the right way at the right time with the right intention, in this world of action, arises.

If we were to profile 'you' as a spiritually intelligent being you would demonstrate the following awareness, attributes and capacities.

You are aware of your self as a spiritual being and no longer would there be any misidentification, beginning with the form that you animate and occupy.

You have the ability to draw on your natural inner resources, your nature, and its attributes of peace, love, joy and wisdom, and to use those resources in the right way in the right moment with the right intention.

You are aware and able to recognise that it is only the ego that sabotages your intelligence when you mistakenly attach your self to some 'thing' that is an image within consciousness, within you, on the screen of your mind.

You are aware of why and how you create a disturbance in your consciousness called emotion, with the ability to identify and name all the emotions that arise today from your attachments yesterday.

You are aware that when you do attach your heart, your self, to any thing (image on your mind), even for a just a few moments, this is also what gives rise to the feeling/perception of separation, disconnection and isolation.

You are aware that any 'insperience' of suffering means you have temporarily lost connection with your true nature which is peace, you have temporarily lost your ability to calibrate the energy of your consciousness and radiate and resonate at the level of love.

You are never surprised or shocked by any event or circumstance as you have realized all that happens 'out there' in the world is exactly what was and is meant to happen.

You are able to see why and how the ego is the 'true cause' of ALL conflict and of any disharmony between people and nations. You are able to use this 'knowingness' in the right way, in the right place at the right time to guide others, and you are therefore never in conflict with anyone.

You never blame others for anything and always accept complete responsibility for your own thoughts, emotions and actions at all times.

You know that you don't have anything to lose as you 'know' that you cannot own or possess anything, hence you are fearless.

You are no longer needy of the approval or the acceptance of others to feel OK about your self, or to be content within your self.

You are free of all dependency, as your sense of security comes from 'inside out' and not 'outside in'.

You have realised that the only way to expand and strengthen your personal capacity to love is to give it, use it, gift it, will it, to others, in the service of others. A service that is therefore often quite subtle.

You see work as a place of creativity, as an opportunity to create new relationships, learn, grow and deepen your self awareness, so that you may understand others better.

You take life lightly, as a game, an opportunity to play, yet you are aware of the significance of time within 'the play'. You are aware, that due to the spiritual virus known as ego, there is a darkness within others and in the world, and that the most effective way to enlighten that darkness for others is to fully liberate your self from it first. You intuitively know that the implicit, invisible and unbreakable connecting energy known as love will do the rest.

Emotional intelligence (EQ)

Notice that whenever you are emotional you are less able to see and do the right thing in the right place at the right moment. In truth, emotions diminish your intelligence. They sabotage your ability to discern, decide and act in the most appropriate and effective ways. Emotion is the energy of 'reaction'. Let's say you become angry at someone, because *they do* what you do not want them to do or *they don't do* what you do want them to do. Your anger is an expression of your ignorance about how 'relationship' with other people works. Anger means you believe you can control others or that others are designed to dance to your tune. Underneath that belief is the belief that others are responsible for your happiness. Wrong on both counts. You are ignorant of the truth that you cannot control another person and no one else is responsible for your happiness.

You then proceed to blame them for what you feel (angry) and express your belief that others make you feel emotionally upset. Wrong again. You do that. You may attempt to justify your anger, saying that it's good and only natural to get angry. Wrong again. If you keep getting angry it will eventually affect your physical health as the scientists now tell us. Plus, you are creating against your own nature which is peaceful and loving. But you will likely find it hard to see your ignorance or lack of intelligence about your emotions and even harder to change what might be the habit of a lifetime, simply because this emotional ignorance is so pervasive. You may even find it hard to see and admit that the anger is sabotaging your rational decision-making.

This of course is why emotional intelligence is, to some extent an oxymoron, a contradiction in terms i.e. when you are emotional it means you are unintelligent.

The beginning of emotional intelligence is gathering information about emotions. It is seeing how emotions are created and caused, and how all emotion is the result of the ego, which is always a case of mistaken identity. A vital aspect of that process is being able to identify and name emotions. That knowledge then allows you to be intelligent (understand other people) when they become emotional and to do the right thing in the right place at the right moment in response.

In the absence of an accurate knowledge and understanding about our emotions, and in the presence of our confusion about our emotions, we learn to believe that love and happiness are emotions. Then, when we associate love and happiness with well-being and good health we come to believe and accept that the emotions that we are mistaking for love and happiness are signs of good health and well-being. When in fact we are creating the opposite and as a consequence we damage our health and sabotage our well being. Then we spend our life searching for some thing, someone, some event or some place to stimulate our emotions from outside our self, and this, as we all know, from first hand experience, lays the foundations in our relationships for something called emotional blackmail.

All of this falls under the heading of 'emotional confusion'. It is a level of confusion that now permeates all societies and all cultures. While there are many areas of confusion, illusion and delusion, these are probably the seven most popular.

Integrated Intelligence

In truth, each of these aspects of intelligence are not separate. They all exist as potential within the consciousness of every human being. They don't sit in separate compartments in our heads. They are interconnected and integrated, and they simply describe the capacity of consciousness, the self, to be intelligent in different ways at different levels.

The Seven Emotional Confusions

As a consequence of our inability to recognize and manage our emotions, we turn love into a business (I'll love you if you love me), happiness into acquisition (I'll be happy when I get.....) and the tears of sadness often become cathartic experience that we confuse with joy (crying at the movies). Then we generate anger and fear when a) love is not returned b) when what we expect and desire fails to arrive or c) when the movie is emotionally boring. And then we wonder why we suffer!

You can see where the saying 'all screwed up' was really intended. In a sense it means ALL of us are all screwed up as we have all inherited and absorbed the same myths/illusions, pass on the same myths/illusions and affirm daily the same myths/illusions. And if we don't react angrily, discuss things fearfully and respond sorrowfully 'on cue', then people start looking at us as if we are from another planet.

Seeing the truth behind an illusion can induce an Aha! moment which is essentially a shift in your perception. This shift disturbs the belief behind the perception, clearing the way to allow the truth to shape the way you perceive/see/feel. And, as the old saying goes, the truth will set you free.

May you see behind the curtain of illusion, see the truth that will banish your delusions, and dissolve all your confusions.

1 Pain is Confused with Pleasure

Though it's hard to believe, it's probably true to say almost every human being learns to believe that pain is pleasure, or that suffering is satisfying, if not sublime. Most of us have been taught to believe that emotions, such as anger, fear and sadness, are healthy and normal, and that our anger is justified. When you create these emotions in response to an event, situation or person, they stimulate the production of certain 'heightening' chemicals in your body, giving the 'illusion' of greater alertness and therefore greater creativity and therefore increased strength. It is these heightening chemicals which can seem to make our emotions pleasurable.

But it's an illusion. These emotions are signs of weakness. If we continue to create them they will, as science has now proved, play a large part in killing our body. This is what we call the psychosomatic factor, where tension and worry create headaches and ulcers, fear and anger contribute towards heart attacks and high blood pressure. Just a few of the 'psychosomatic' consequences of such emotions.

We are born into a world which accepts and teaches us that fear and anger are natural and necessary experiences within all our relationships. It is this prevalent belief that 'emotion' is healthy, which gives us the convenient excuse not to do something about understanding and changing them. We justify creating them by recalling parents and teachers, plus our role models in life, as people who demonstrated how to create and express them. We mimic them, first in our head, then in our actions.

These emotions are obviously uncomfortable. It's only after they have passed that there may be the feeling of relief, which is then associated with some kind of happiness. But its not real happiness, just relief from our self-created stress. Stress (the emotions of fear, anger and sadness) is simply a message saying there is something you need to change. It is saying something is out balance, out of harmony, within you. Not within others or the world, but within you. So the first thing that needs to be changed is the belief that someone else is making you emote anger or fear, that someone else is causing your emotional stress. No they aren't. This is good news, as it means you can do something about what many people believe is outside of their control. The second thing to be changed is the belief that the world and people out there can be controlled. It can't. They can't. The third thing that needs to change is the belief that others are responsible for our happiness, for our 'feelings'. No their not. It's an inside job!

"PLEASURE is knowing who you are and accepting life as it is because you no longer need to pretend to be someone that you are not, you no longer attempt to control anyone else or attempt to acquire something in order to get what you already have!"

I Was so Moved!

It's a saying we use when something or someone seems to touch us and we become quite emotional. "Wasn't it so touching," is often heard after funerals, after movies, after the honest confessions of another or at the sight of something beautiful in nature. They can all seem to move us to tears or to joy, to a state where we feel overcome by some 'emotion'. I hope you are sitting comfortably. Ultimately, from the spiritual point of view, which is knowing and understanding that spirit is what you are, they are all just emotional indulgences. They are signs of weakness within the self. Why? Because they are saying that 'you' are not moving you, you are allowing something or someone outside your self to move you. You are bringing that something or someone from outside your self, putting them/it up on the screen of your mind, attaching your self to them/it and losing your self in them/it. So it's not an empowering experience. Quite the opposite, it's a sign that you are still dependent. Now you are probably thinking, "My God, is nothing out there meant to touch me? Isn't it going to be a cold, hard, isolated existence, in which nothing I see can move me"? No, actually quite the opposite. Still watch, still see, still appreciate something of beauty, but instead of being moved by it, which means you are taking from it, give to it, move towards it, and give to it, give your appreciation. Extend the energy of you, which is love, as you appreciate what you see. As you bless what you see. As you applaud what you see. This is love in action. You will feel the power of love, the power of you, is moving you. And you will know that you are once again the master of your life because you are love. Are you the moved or the mover?

2 Stimulation is Confused with Relaxation

It's the end of another busy day. You arrive home and it's time to relax. Out comes that big sigh of relief and up go the feet in front of the TV, and the only movement for the next few hours will be a finger on the remote. It's the midnight movie and it's Rambo III. Ninety minutes worth of stress, terror, horror, wall-to-wall violence and the occasional splattering of blood. But are you really relaxing? Or are you being stimulated? Is it relaxation or stimulation?

We have been brilliantly conditioned to believe that hanging out in front of the TV or going to the movie is a good way to relax. But it's not relaxation, it's stimulation. And stimulation is not relaxation, it's stimulation. As you use your mental energy to process the energy coming through your eyes and ears you drain your power. The presence of any 'on screen' emotion captures your attention, draws you in and, before you know it, you begin to generate the exact same emotional state within your self, albeit at a lesser intensity.

Watch yourself as you watch others on the flickering screen. Watch yourself being 'sucked into' the drama of the movie or the soap and begin to live through the characters. Whatever they feel, you feel. They become excited and you become excited. They become sad and you become sad. The entertainment industry relies on you to surrender your consciousness, and therefore your life, for a couple of hours at least, to the characters which they create. They manipulate you through your mind and it's as if you allow them to do the work of thinking and feeling for you. And you even pay them to do it!

You create and fill your conscious and subconscious with unhealthy, negative energy (words and images) and then, when real life resumes, you wonder why you can't be more optimistic and positive in real life. You sit with your eyes wide open, while the discerning eye of your consciousness, your intellectual faculty, stays wide shut.

True relaxation is being free of all stimulation. For the mind it is silence, for the emotions it is stillness, for the body it is motionlessness, without a trace of tension or the tightening of any muscle. Real relaxation is the release of all tension. Not so easy if you are addicted to watching and absorbing the tensions and the tears of others dramas, which are not even real.

Relaxation is an art and a science. But the marketing men have been so clever they have convinced us that stimulation is relaxation. It is a neat ploy that keeps their hand in your pocket. But although they seem to know what they are doing they know not what they do.

> **RELAXATION is the absence of all physical tension,**
> **mental anxiety and spiritual ignorance.**
> **It is the presence of a healthy body,**
> **mental alertness and a well being.**

 ## Creative Capacity

Don't get me wrong. I am not saying go home and throw out your TV. However it makes sense to be careful with your relationship with technology. Essentially technology is designed to mimic and duplicate the functions of consciousness, i.e. create images, project images, record (memorise) images, replay images, edit images, manipulate images and re-present images in a variety of ways. These are all faculties of human creativity, and when we allow technology to do the work for us, our creative capacity atrophies and we become lazy. This is obviously why the media can be so easily used to influence millions of minds, which is essentially the manipulation of emotion. It's not a conspiracy, it's just the way the game of life on earth has evolved. Only it's not evolution in a progressive sense. It's evolution in a regressive sense. In the sense that we are not waking up each day and becoming clearer, freer, wiser, more self empowered. Quite the opposite, generally speaking

3 Revenge is Confused with Joy

To celebrate the pain of others is obviously somewhat perverted. But it sits at the heart of what we call a good story or a good movie. To feel joy at the comeuppance of 'the baddie' is now one of our most prevalent emotional confusions. Sometimes, as a way of justifying our 'joyful revenge', we call it justice. Script writers, novelists and journalists all use this confusion to hook us into their stories.

Revenge is driven by hate at worst and mild anger at best. Retribution is its game and celebration is its aim. Revenge says, "I really enjoyed it when they got a 'dose of their own medicine'... I was so happy to see them suffer for what they had done." It is a perversion of joy that can only sustain our misery. Unless we bring to an end our inner production line of anger and hate towards others, we will simply live a very unhappy and unhealthy life.

The urge towards revenge and its celebration can only end when the belief, that others are responsible for what you feel, is seen to be an illusion. Only when you take full responsibility for whatever emotion you create and feel will it be possible to end the anger and the hate that's seeks revenge. Only when your self image, based on the belief 'I am a victim', is shattered and replaced with the truth that 'I am never a victim' will you cease to point the finger at others for whatever hurt you may feel.

Only when it is fully seen and accepted that 'no one can hurt me... ever (you can hurt my body but not me), will rage become extinct and desire for revenge a relic of the past. Only when love is known and shaped into compassion for both the victim and the abuser will it be possible to be totally free of all judgment, condemnation and any desire to see and take pleasure from justice done.

Only then will it be possible to rediscover true joy in life, because as long as there is even the slightest sense of celebration at the suffering that is inflicted upon others, even upon 'the perpetrator', as long as there is a thrill at revenge being delivered, true joy can never be known or lived. And life is designed for joy to be present, for joy to burst forth like spring flowers, for joy to celebrate the very gift of living. Life without true joy is not living, it's only surviving, tolerating and continuously battling a virus called reluctance.

> **Joy is the gurgling, bubbling, effervescent energy of your life bursting through you and out into the world.**
> **You can only feel joy and be joyful when your heart is free from all fear, anger and sadness.**

Don't Express, Suppress or Repress

While you may acknowledge that fear and anger are unhealthy don't try to do what many attempt, which is to suppress them. These emotions will come. **Emotion is the price you pay today for your attachments yesterday.** *You've spent your whole life creating your attachments which are always the origins of your emotion, so it's going to take a little time to heal the habit of attaching and thereby ceasing to generate these emotions. The first step is simply acknowledging them as unhealthy, unwanted and unnecessary. But don't resist them when they come. If you resist them you will suppress them. And if you continue to suppressing your emotions i.e. pushing them down, you may become what is often called 'repressed'. At the same time don't express them otherwise you may do something you will regret. Simply watch them. And they will pass. As they must.* **All emotion dies under observation.** *And the more inwardly skilled you become at observing them the weaker they become until one day they come no more. At which point you will have arrived 'home' and reside once again in your true nature which is free of all emotion.*

4 Worry is confused with Care

Were you blessed with a fretting parent? Perhaps as a teenager you only had to be ten minutes late home and your mother would not be shy in letting you know her exact emotional state. "Where have you been, I've been so worried about you, why didn't you call to say you were going to be late? You know I always worry." To which you probably replied, "Stop worrying about me mother, I'm OK, why are you ALWAYS worrying?"

To which your mother is likely to have said, "But you know I WORRY because I CARE." In those eight words, you learned two fatal lessons that would likely haunt you for the rest of your life. The first is that worry equals care. No it doesn't. Worry is fear and care is love, and the two can never meet. Fear always chases love away.

The second fatal lesson is the idea that it's good to worry! The moment you inherit the belief that worry is a good demonstration that you care you will delude yourself into believing that it's important to show others that you worry about others in particular and world events in general. Otherwise people might think you don't care. And the last thing you want is to be seen to be heartless. This will eventually make you look for something to worry about, and, when you cannot find anything to worry about, you worry, because there's nothing to worry about! How strange and perverse is our life, when we feel uncomfortable if we are not feeling uncomfortable.

So if you are the parent, what would be a better way to respond? Have you ever picked up the phone to find the person calling was someone you were thinking about a few moments earlier? Ever said something and the other person said, "I was just thinking the same thing"? We are all linked at a subtle, invisible level, with the capacity to connect and communicate with others invisibly. We do 'pick up' the energy that others radiate, especially the ones that we are close to.

So let's say your teenage family member is out late and didn't phone home. They will pick up on your subtle energy. You have no idea what situation they are in at any and every moment. Speculation is futile and a waste of your energy. If you worry then you are sending them the vibrations of fear, a negative energy, which doesn't empower them but is more likely to distract them. Perhaps they are in a tricky situation and only they can decide how they will navigate through it. What will help them, what will support and empower them most? Your vibration of anger at not receiving their call? Your vibration of fear as you imagine something bad has happened? Or the vibrations of your unconditional love and your good wishes.

What will you send them? Worry vibrations or the vibrations of love in the form of your good wishes for them? Besides, when you worry about someone else, who are you really worried about?

CARE is you extending your self to connect with and embrace another with the light of your being.
You can only be care full when you are empty of all self concern.

 What a Worry!

Not only do many of us worry our way through life but the tension and anxiety that emanates from the centre of all our worries becomes addictive. Instead of giving thanks for our blessings each day, it's as if some people give thanks for their daily worries! When it's suggested that it may not be a positive use of time and energy, the worry addict will say, "But it's good to worry. It's necessary to worry, so that we can prepare for the worst." They can't quite see how their belief, that worry is a good preparation for the worst, is blinding them to the truth that all worry is simply miscreation. It is to misuse the creative capacity of our consciousness. For what is worry but 'fantasized catastrophizing', it is to create an image of the worst possible outcome on the screen of your mind and then use that image to frighten the living daylights out of your self. And besides when you worry who are you really worried about? Your self. You are worried about what you will feel if something bad actually happens. In truth, worry is selfish, but we justify it by calling it caring. Some even base their personal identity on a 'worry profile.' "Yes I am a worrier, I have always been a worrier, I guess I must have inherited it from my parents, it's probably in my genes". Not true. Worry is just another learned mental habit. It can be unlearned. On the 'other side' of worry there is peace.

5 Anger is Confused with Assertion

Maybe you had an angry parent, who used their anger to manipulate and motivate you to do what they wanted. Maybe your teacher at school used anger to control the classroom, or at least appear to. Maybe you have an angry boss whose rages around the office, seems to get people moving. Or maybe you see our politicians or our media becoming angry and it seems to achieve some kind of positive change.

In each of the above, we learn another fatal lesson which only increases our emotional confusion - that anger is the way to assert yourself, motivate others and create change for the better. In a world filled with people who have learned to become stubborn, defensive and inflexible, sometimes it seems that anger is the only way to motivate them, incite them to action, challenge them to change, so it is muddled with assertiveness. But anger is never assertive as it is filled with resentment and resentment only begets resistance, thus losing any capacity to influence the kind of positive change that will endure.

Using anger in the workplace is the lazy man's way to manage others. It is a form of emotional blackmail that says, "I will be angry at you if you don't…" It is an obvious attempt to induce fear in the other, in the hope that it will motivate the other. Most parents will find it hard to resist the temptation to use anger to control the child's behaviour. Besides, anger is the most destructive emotion which usually does its greatest damage to its creator. All you have to do is be a little self aware when you are angry and you will see that you are the one who suffers first and most.

Some see anger as the emotion which is justified by the apparent absence of justice. This is what they call righteous anger, but it only delays the arrival of natural justice which moves at its own speed and is usually out of sight until the moment of it's arrival. To rage against injustice is to forget that everything happens for a reason, every effect has a cause and whatever has happened is exactly what was meant to happen.

In the case of any physical disease, a cure is not possible until the cause is fully known and treated. Unfortunately anger doesn't have time for understanding and healing. By identifying with the pain or the plight of others, or taking offence at an insult towards the self, anger only sustains our own pain under the illusion that we are being assertive, that we are doing something about it, that we are reacting in the right way.

Passion also becomes a grey area when anger interferes with meaning. Sometimes we say, "I am so passionate about this cause because I am so angry." But anger can never be passion. Authentic passion is enthusiasm. And the difference between anger and enthusiasm is one always drains your energy while the other energises you, one blinds you to a positive course of action while the other gives you the clarity to see the right way forward, one is impatient and out of balance while the other is patient and centered.

And then there are those who just get angry at another's anger, believing that it is the only way to balance things out and make things right. Sometimes it's called war. They are under the illusion that two negatives make a positive. Now where might we have learned that?

> **You can only be ASSERTIVE when you cease to**
> **react emotionally to the actions of others,**
> **when you cease to diminish your self in any way,**
> **when you bear no grudges and end all blame.**

A Dream of Peace

All anger is directed backwards. It is also a futile attempt to change what has already happened. Unfortunately it clouds our ability to work creatively with the moment now, so that the future can be more positive. People will even begin to get angry at the idea that anger is useless and that there is no place for anger in their world. They are already getting angry at the past that they will have in the future! All the while they may even continue to say peace is good, peace is what they seek. But they don't realise how their belief in anger will always be the main obstacle to finding peace in their own life. That's why 'fighting for peace' is an oxymoron.

6 Fear is Confused with Respect

Often our emotional confusion begins with the wrong use of language. A bully can normally be found in the playground of most schools and in many offices. The bully wants people to fear him or her, but they will call it respect. They demand that others respect them and yet they attempt to induce fear. We learn to confuse fear with respect early in life.

Even the leaders of nations can be heard to say that we must respect another nation when what they really mean is fear them. It is impossible to give respect to another if we, in our own minds, fear them. If you are scared of someone or something, it means there is an absence of self -respect and, if you do not respect your self, you cannot truly respect another. It is only when you stand in the armour of your own self-respect that you have no fear of others and are then capable of giving genuine respect to others.

Somehow, somewhere along the way, our language has twisted and confused the meanings of fear and respect. Sometimes we become fearful of being seen as being fearful, so we try to avoid admitting we fear someone by saying we respect them, and suddenly the real meaning of respect is lost. It's not hard to understand that probably the most important education in life is how to restore and maintain our self-respect. It's no coincidence that almost all forms of abuse, crime and destructive behaviour can be traced back to a lack of self-respect. If we don't have respect for ourselves, we will look for it from others and eventually demand it from others. Unable to recognize it in ourselves we are therefore unable to recognize it in others. Simply getting someone's attention is then mistaken for being respected. And if we don't receive it we will try to induce it using a variety of subtle and not so subtle methods. Suddenly we become the bully ourselves.

When you realize that it's the absence of self-respect that is one of the main factors that is attracting the aggression of others you begin to take greater responsibility for the energy you are emitting. But it's hard to see that it's our self that we need to work on, and not the bully that needs to be fixed. That essentially means freeing ourselves from the fear of others. That is only possible when you find your inner worth and begin to esteem your self. And that is only possible when you correct your self image, where you stop identifying with a negative self image. And that is only possible by realising who you really are, and what you really are. And that, as we have seen, is exactly what we don't know. When we needed to know there was no-one who could teach us. Self-worth and self-respect were not, and generally are still not, on the curriculum.

It's quite possible that one country will go to war with another because one or two leaders have a lack of self-respect. They will probably be brilliant at disguising it and quite masterful in putting on the masks of self-confidence and self-worth. But if their self-respect were genuine, they would not be scared for themselves or anyone else, and they would have the courage and the patience to work with, talk with, engage with, listen to and offer the hand of friendship to anyone and everyone including so called adversaries. But when they don't have the strength of their own self-respect and when they are unaware of their lack of self-respect, fear will have its way. And that's why the restoration of self-respect is only possible when the ego is recognized and no longer sustained. Because, as we saw earlier, fear always comes from the ego or, in the language of New Scotland Yard, from yet another a case of mistaken identity.

**To RESPECT another is to acknowledge and affirm
the innate goodness and worth of the other
regardless of their actions in the present or in the past.**

 It's Not BAD!

It's easy to get the impression that this approach to understanding emotion implies that emotions are bad and should not happen. Nothing could be further from the truth. If you start to think that way then it just leads to self blame and further suppression. Emotion is just a signal that you are out of alignment with the authentic self, the real you. It's a lifetime habit, and those habits are buried deep in your subconscious. So you are not going to wake up one day and suddenly be without all emotion and 100% loving, joyful and contented. If you do, please let me know, I want to know how to did it!

7 Sadness is Confused with Love

Picture yourself in the record store. You are browsing the CDs. You spot a new CD with all the greatest love songs at a knock-down, bargain-basement, special sale price. You can't resist. Once home it's time for your musical 'love in' with just you and the CD. You arrange the room carefully. Candles in the corner, box of chocolates on one side and a box of tissues on the other. Down go the lights and up comes the music. It's not long before your eyes are watering and the tears roll down your cheeks as you fall under the spell of the songs of sadness, believing they are songs of love.

You wallow for an hour in musically-induced sentiment and melancholy, perhaps thinking and hoping that, one day, you too will find such love in a profoundly special and tearful relationship with someone in the world, or wondering why you haven't yet!

Later that evening, it's off to the movies. It's a love story designed to pluck every string in your heart. The hero and his heroine, or the heroine and her hero, journey together through a well-worn formula. First the meeting of the eyes, then the first kiss, the first row, the first making up, the first serious mistake, the first forgiveness. In just over an hour, you have accompanied them through a rainbow of emotions. One minute you are shedding tears, the next minute you are clapping, then raging against misfortune and then celebrating triumph against adversity. And then you find your self thinking if only YOU could experience so much love in life in such a short time. You conclude the evening by thinking how mundane and boring your own life seems. Then it's the final scene. The embrace, the kiss, the sunset, the music, the silhouettes, as the tears cascade down your face and your nose requires half a box of tissues!

If you were to consult a psychiatrist at precisely that moment, you would probably be certified as clinically depressed. But this is love ... isn't it? OK I exaggerate ... a little. But I'm sure you get the picture. Our music and entertainment industries have brilliantly conditioned us to confuse sadness with love, which is like confusing black with white and down with up. The love song and the love story are filled with sorrow, which we then mistakenly identify with the jewel in the crown of the human spirit - love. Perhaps there is no greater illusion in life than sadness is love! Perhaps there is no greater emotional addiction than the sadness that signifies we are feeling sorry for our self. It becomes a comfort blanket, like the one we had as a baby, that we carry around with us everywhere, refusing to be parted from it. Poor me. Perhaps that's why even when you hear people laughing and talking happily, if you listen closely, behind their laughter, underneath their apparent happiness, you can hear their sadness.

LOVE is what you are, what everyone is, regardless of your thoughts, and feelings now or in the past. It is only known when there is no longer any impulse towards separation and when all sense of 'mine' has gone.

Emotional Addiction

Attributing our sadness to the words and actions of others is what a huge part of our entertainment industry is built upon. Accumulated and suppressed moments of sadness, that have built up over time at home or in the office, get a chance to 'break out' of our consciousness to see the light of day. The movie and the TV soap are triggers. This of course is known as catharsis. The relief, that is felt when the burden of our depression is released is confused with happiness and creates its own addiction. Being addicted to sorrow and sadness sounds strange, but it is as real as any other addiction. Subconsciously we even look for reasons to be sad and then, when we do create sad, we suppress it. Over time, we build up a stock of sorrow so we can indulge either in a long sulk as we feel sorry for our self, or a tearful bursting of our emotional dam, often triggered by that famous 'last straw' that breaks the famous camel's back. But it is all just the egos game, a game in which it keeps itself alive. All emotion can always be traced back to our old friend the ego or mistaken identity. If there were no attachment there would be no sense of loss and therefore no sadness or sorrow and therefore the constant presence of authentic happiness. You don't need to search for happiness, just drop all the sorrow and sadness. Easy...yes?

How do you FEEL?

So much for emotion…for now. But what about feeling? Having explored both the mechanism and nature of ego/attachment as the source and the ground from which all our emotions arise, where love, happiness, peace, joy, contentment are NOT emotions but states of being, what then of feeling? What is feeling?

Is there a difference between emotion and feeling, and why are we almost as equally confused about our feelings as we are about our emotions? When we ask each other 'how do you feel' what we really mean is what are you feeling right now. But how do we feel, what is happening exactly when we say 'I feel'? Is it possible to not feel what we are feeling? Can we choose our feelings? And if not why not, if so, how?

The most essenceful definition:

FEELING is:..

Perception by Touch

This makes sense when you realize that each one of us can feel/perceive/ touch at three levels – physical, mental/intellectual and spiritual.

Physical Feeling

When you go to a department store, you don't wait for the dress or the suit to come to you. You go to it. And you **touch** it and, as you touch it, you **feel** it. As you feel the texture you **perceive** the quality of the cloth, you **feel/perceive** the width, by **touching** it. You are using your physical senses to touch/feel/perceive something, so you would obviously call this a 'physical feeling'.

Mental/Intellectual Feeling

As you have been reading this book, your mind has been open (thank you!) and you have been taking in the insights and ideas here through the window of your mind, given them life on the screen of your mind and then perceived (looked at) them with your intellect. While your mind is like a screen and a window, and the first faculty of consciousness, your intellect is that second faculty, which you use to discern quality, appropriateness, trueness, and then make decisions. Intellect is what separates us from the plant and animal kingdoms. It gives us the ability to philosophise, reflect, evaluate and design, and then bring our designs to life at a physical level. Our intellect gives us the ability to make choices across the spectrum from the rational to the intuitive.

So as you perceive an idea or insight, it's as if you touch it, you perceive it, you feel it, with your intellect. And as you do, your head nods and a little voice inside says, "I get that. That feels logical. I see/I perceive the logic in that."

In that instance, it's as if you are using your **rational** ability to feel/perceive the rightness of an idea. But sometimes you don't perceive/see the rightness rationally and yet still your head nods a 'yes', and the voice inside says, "Yes, I get that, I don't see the reason for that, but I tell you what, it just 'feels right'. It rings a bell." In that moment you are using your **intuitive** ability to feel/touch/perceive the rightness of something.

Can you see the difference? We can all feel/perceive at either end of the intellectual spectrum – the rational end and the intuitive end – they are simply the two ends of the same spectrum, and although they fire up different parts of the brain (left for rational and right for intuitive - according to our brainy scientist friends) from the point of view of the one conscious entity that you are, they are on the same continuum within your consciousness.

You can easily develop your 'perceptual feeling' at the intellectual level. Write down a current problem that you believe you are facing. Then create seven possible solutions/responses/ways forward, regardless of how crazy or weird they may seem at first. Then, once the list is complete contemplate each possibility and notice how you are using your intellectual capacity to assess and evaluate the quality and practicality of each. Notice how you are not just thinking about each one but feeling for the quality, the appropriateness of each. And as you watch how you feel about each, possibility you will also notice other possibilities emerging during the contemplative/feeling/perceiving process.

It is this lack of intellectual development, or lack of awareness of the function, capacity and power of our intellect, that impairs our evaluation and decision-making ability. Hence the reason so many of us become stressed when we have to make decisions. Unfortunately no one ever teaches us in our formal education, how to properly develop our full range of 'perceiving/feeling' at the intellectual level. The reason is simple. When we were at school they only wanted the third faculty of your consciousness, of you, which was your memory. We learned to believe that memorizing was learning, but it isn't, it's just memorizing. Real learning is the development of thinking and feeling/perceiving skills involving our mind and intellect. But those big people, who taught us, didn't really know any better, because no one taught them about the true functions of their mind and intellect. Once again, no-one is to blame, but we are all responsible...as they say!

Spiritual Feeling

Your deepest capacity to feel is at the spiritual level. Has there ever been someone in your life who, as soon they stepped through the door of home, without seeing them, you knew the exact mood they were in? Sometimes they could be in another building and you sensed the mood they were in. How? Because you picked up what we have come to call 'their vibrations'. In other words you pick up the transmission of the radiant energy that they are.

We are all transmitting energy at all times. And that energy is totally invisible and intangible. It's as if you could feel their presence at a subtle, invisible level. Those who 'believe' they have fallen in love know this well. All they can think about is each other. They intensely transmit their vibration, their thoughts, to each other, because they are thinking about each other and they pick up (feel) each other's feelings, even when they are far apart.

But the deepest spiritual feeling is not picking up and feeling the vibrations (radiant energy) of others. Anywhere and at any time, you can make the journey of no distance in one second and focus your attention into your self. It's there that you will perceive your peace, you will feel your peace, you will touch and feel the peace that you are, that you always are, at the heart of your being.

All you have to do is practice ignoring any external noises (including other people, until you perfect your inward journey), pay no attention to any stray thoughts or waves of emotion that pass through your consciousness and go straight to the heart of your consciousness, which is you. In truth you are already there because you cannot be anywhere else. And there, in your heart, your real heart, in YOU, you will perceive, touch, feel... your peace. Because peace is the true and abiding nature of you. It is you.

Could it be that simple? Yes it could. So why don't we do it, why don't we feel it, why do we 'believe' we can't? Again the answer is so simple when you see it... when you perceive it!

Two Fatal Lessons

When you were young, you were taught that feeling is a noun, but it's not, it's a verb. You were taught that feelings happen to you instead of something that you do. You were taught that feelings were more like things that had to be sought and acquired, not something that you create. Do you remember the first time your mother or father took you to see your first circus or football match or big event? As your mum sat there next to you, she said, "Isn't this exciting, I am so happy and excited, excited and happy. Aren't you excited and happy, aren't you happy and excited." Or something to that effect. You were of course excited. So you looked up at Mum as if to say, "Yes I am excited and happy, happy and excited." In those moments your parent/s, or whatever big person you were with, taught you two fatal lessons. The first fatal lesson was that excitement equals happiness. No it doesn't. Excitement is what happens to the water in a kettle when it boils. The molecules are agitated. When you are excited, you are agitated. But agitation is not happiness. It's agitation. Happiness for a human being is contentment and a natural flow of joy moving freely through your 'being' and out into the world. That's happiness. Not agitation, not excitement.

The second fatal lesson in this common parent/child scene was that your feelings in life have to come from outside your self. And when you believe that your feelings in life have to come from outside you, what do you spend the rest of your life doing? Searching for some kind of stimulation, searching outside yourself for what you believe will give you the feeling of happiness. The destiny of someone who is always looking for stimulation is dependency and eventually addiction. Which explains why almost all of us are addicted to something, someone or somewhere. This is why, deep down inside, so many of us lead what has been called lives of quiet desperation. It's impossible to find real peace, love or happiness outside your self. Yet almost our entire belief system is founded on such an illusion.

But now you know (in theory at least) that they are your natural states of being. They are your nature. Always only one second and no distance away.

States of Being
So there you have it. Emotions always have their origin in ego. They arise as a result of the attachment to and identification with something that you are not. When something 'happens to' what you attach to and identify with, it then feels like it's happening to you. But it's not. Emotion is the price you pay today for your attachments yesterday. Emotions cloud and confuse. Any

time you 'react' to anything or anyone, it means emotion is present. It means you have lost control, lost mastery, of your own energy and the emotion (that you create) takes over and is controlling you until it subsides.

Love, peace and happiness, on the other hand, are not emotions as we have defined emotion here. They are very real and dynamic states of being. They are not agitations or stimulations, they are what you are, by nature. They are what you are able to emit but only when you are free of attachment. They are your natural states, which then inform your intentions, thoughts and actions, but only when you are not making the mistake of identifying with something that you are not, only when you are free of that desire for something in return.

Peace is what you are by nature, love is what radiates from you naturally, and happiness, in the form of joy, is what you feel when no attachment blocks or distorts your radiant nature. They are the core constituents or states of YOU and they can never be taken away from you. You get to decide and choose what state to create, to 'be in', but you sabotage that choice by 'attaching' and thereby distorting your energy, you, into emotions such as fear, anger and sadness and their many forms and faces.

This is why they (peace, love and happiness) are sometimes referred to as your inheritance. But in truth, you don't inherit them because you cannot inherit what is already there. If you simply remember who and what you are, cease to identify with any thing that you are not, you will naturally be able to create and feel these states again. You will be free to fully choose your feelings again.

When you are at peace, notice, you are not agitated so there is no emotion. When you are at peace, in your peace, you 'feel' peace. Notice that when you are love, when you give of your self without wanting anything in return, there is no agitation, there is no emotion, just the smooth movement from intention to the action of giving, free of expectation (attachment). And when you give with love, you feel love…ing. Notice when you are genuinely happy, you are contented and smiling with a quiet joy. Your life energy, which is you, is flowing out into the world around you without stimulation or agitation, there is no emotion. And as you radiate your own personal version of contentment and joy, notice what you feel. You feel contented and joyful. No agitation. No emotion.

But it's as if it's been so long since we were without emotion, it's been so long since we have become addicted to our agitations, that it's hard to imagine let alone feel that life without emotion is more natural and true than life as an emotional rollercoaster.

Feeling Your Emotions

So let's finally bring emotions and feelings together, because you do 'feel' your emotions. You scratch my car and I get angry. (I haven't read this book yet!) There is a moment in my angriness when I turn to you and say, "I feel angry."

In that moment, I am beginning to separate my self from the anger that I have created. In that moment it's as if I am saying there is 'me' and there is 'anger', and I am feeling, touching, perceiving the anger 'in here', in me. In effect I am detaching from the emotion that I have created and am now consciously perceiving/feeling the anger. If I keep detaching, not avoiding, not suppressing, but just pulling back and acknowledging there is me and there is the anger, and that I 'feel' it, then the anger dissipates and dies. All emotion dies under observation. That's because the emotion is essentially an illusion. It's not real.

How can emotion be an illusion when it feels so real? Remember that emotion comes from EGO, always. And the ego is attachment to and identification with something that is not the true me. Ego is therefore the 'seat of illusion', the source of an identity that is not real, not true. So the ego's product or progeny, which is emotion, is not real. As long as you keep identifying with what you are not, the emotion will seem real. But as soon as you come away from the emotion and just look at it, inwardly observe it, it's as if you are coming back to what is real within you, to what is the true you, a source of love, a source of peace, a source of joy. It's as if you are coming back to the centre where you always find your peace and your power. And when you are in this, your true state, then the illusion is dispelled, which is why the emotions dies.

Next time you are driving home along a misty road, try to grab a handful of mist. You can't, it's not there. It just looks as if something is there, until you attempt to grasp it. So it is with emotion. It's the ghost that ultimately has no power over you, but only after you have learned to see it as a ghost, like a rolling mist across the landscape of your consciousness. But to do that it is necessary to be your self, your true self, and bring an end to all attachment/misidentification.

Emotions Kill Your Capacity to Feel

Too much chilli in your food too often over a period of time will diminish your capacity to taste. Too many glasses of alcohol or too many injections of addictive drugs, over time, will sabotage your capacity to control your own thoughts. Too many emotional disturbances, over time, will severely diminish your capacity to feel.

Imagine you are surrounded by a group of friends at home, or perhaps colleagues at work. In mid-group conversation, someone says something that triggers an emotional reaction in you. You are upset and you create anger. You are agitated. You are experiencing an emotional upheaval/ agitation within. All you can feel is your own upsetness.

As the conversation continues, you cannot choose to change your feelings. All you can feel is your emotional upheaval. As one friend/ colleague speaks of their recent family loss, you cannot choose to create, feel and be empathic. You are in the grip of your upsetness, your anger. When another admits to a huge mistake that affected the whole group's work, you cannot choose to create, feel and give forgiveness. Your anger is still alive in your consciousness, and still distracting you and distorting your energy. It has almost all your attention. When another explains the incredible pain they are feeling after a recent fall you cannot choose to create, feel and give compassion. And when someone reports the birth of a new child you cannot choose to create, feel and give happiness.

Why? Because you are totally caught in the inner storm of your own emotional disturbance. That's all that you can 'feel', until the emotional storm subsides. When you are emotional ALL that you can 'feel' is that emotion. It's not as if you are choosing to be 'emotional', it is simply the ruler of your consciousness in those moments, until it subsides. The cause is, as we saw earlier, is always an image that you are attached to and identified with on your own mind.

What can easily happen next is that instead of detaching and just observing the emotion that you 'feel' and thereby disempowering it, instead of taking responsibility for your creation and thereby resolving it, you try to push it down. You suppress it. Why? Because you want to return your full attention to the group, engage with the group and be able to respond appropriately. So you suppress. The emotion is then stored in your subconscious.

Over time, the habitually suppressed emotions build up in the inner shelves of your subconscious and then, one day, you explode in an emotional outburst, which to others has no rhyme or reason, and then you start to wonder what is wrong with you. Or perhaps you find your self in a therapy group or a breakout group in the middle of a workshop, and you start to share the emotions that you felt in such situations and, as you talk, you feel the arising of those emotions again. You begin to let what has been stored out of the store. You allow it to well up and pour out. You tell all. And then, when you're done, those in the group might say, "Thank you for sharing, you spoke from the heart," which seemed to affirm that it was good to be emotional, which then becomes 'emotion is good', which then becomes 'emotion is normal', it's healthy. When in fact, in reality, it's the opposite. It's a sign of something abnormal, something unnatural and unhealthy. It's not bad, simply a signal that you are not thinking, feeling and acting in alignment with the true you.

It's a sign that the ego has taken over and is in control. It wasn't the heart that spoke, but the ego that dumped. But you leave the group therapy believing you did the right thing, you 'feel' healed, but in truth you are more likely to discover it was just a temporary relief, as you eased the subconscious pressure of your built-up emotions. It was cathartic.

Instead of tracing the emotion back to its cause and transforming it, thereby restoring the energy of the self to its natural state, we tend to either express or suppress. In both cases the emotion is recorded, it becomes a file in the filing cabinet of memory, a file that is then pulled at the drop of the 'proverbial hat' in the future, triggering the recreation of the recorded emotion as it pours out again.

Its expression or suppression then becomes a strand (habit) in the 'cloak of many colours' known as your personality. And because you learn to believe you are your personality, you start to identify your self with your emotional creations, which are really miscreations. And the cycle is closed. You are trapped. The ego is now using it's own creation to find another new false identity.

When the ego is recognized as the source of your emotions you will also start to see the full range of emotions that you create. This 'seeing' and growing ability to identify your emotions is essential in restoring self mastery. With practice you will start to check your self before becoming attached, and thereby consciously choose not to create and feel emotional. You can then start to cut back on your emotional addictions, which almost all emotions tend to become. Here is why.

The Cycle of Emotion is the Cycle of Suffering

Essentially there are three families of emotion which means three kinds of agitation, three kinds of disturbances, that you create and feel in your consciousness when you identify with something that you are not. They are sadness, anger and fear and they work in perfect circular harmony. Why do you create and feel **sadness**? It's always because you believe that you have lost something. Sadness always follows a sense of loss. If, over time, you 'believe' you have many losses and therefore create many moments of sadness, depression will set in. Have you ever noticed that when you create sadness, the sadness doesn't last (unless there is depression). It passes, like all emotion must.

However, as sadness passes, it turns, turns and turns, into **anger**, as you seek to blame someone or something for your loss, for your sorrow, for your emotional pain. So you look for someone or something on which to project your pain. You start to play the blame game. But the anger too will also pass. Try getting angry and staying angry. It's impossible. You'll start laughing after a while at the ridiculousness of it, or you'll just get tired.

Then, as the anger passes it turns, turns and turns into **fear**. You create the fear that it might happen again, that you might experience loss again. A new worry is born. Worry is fear. And guess what will happen if you create the thought that loss will happen? It will happen, as it must, in a world where we are taught to attach to things that must inevitable come and go. When it does happen you will create and feel sadness. The sadness will turn into anger and the anger into fear, and so on.

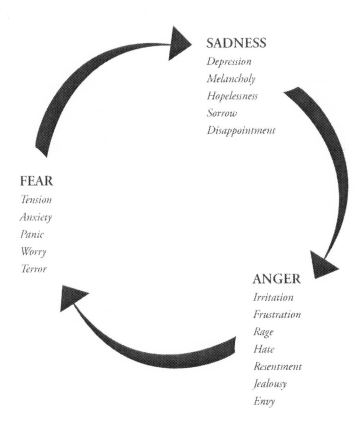

SADNESS
Depression
Melancholy
Hopelessness
Sorrow
Disappointment

FEAR
Tension
Anxiety
Panic
Worry
Terror

ANGER
Irritation
Frustration
Rage
Hate
Resentment
Jealousy
Envy

This is not only the *cycle of emotion* it is the *cycle of suffering*. Yet our education systems teach it, governments sustain it, economies depend, companies profit from it and there would not be an entertainment industry if we did not become addicted to our own emotional creations. You could almost see it as a conspiracy to keep us all preoccupied with our emotional suffering. It's just that the ones who would be conspiring are creating and living in the same cycle! Yes, there may interludes of real peace, real love and real happiness. But they will be very brief, simply because the culture of the world is 'set up' to keep us in this cycle of emotion, believing that it is the way to live.

All 'emotions' will find their way into one of the three families of emotion or a combination of two or three. The only way to break the cycle is to realize that you have nothing to lose, which means to realize that you can never possess anything in the first place. It's the attachment to your belief that you can possess things that is the cause of your attempt to possess things, which in turn is the cause of your attachment/misidentification which is the cause of your mental/emotional suffering!

Breaking out of the cycle of suffering will not be possible until you realize what you are 'in truth'. As long as you think you are only a material, physical being, and all the other labels that come with it, then your primary reality will be the material, physical world around you. And along with that comes the idea, the belief, that you can own or possess some of that material reality.

The foundations of our society are built on the belief in possession and ownership. But the moment you know yourself as a being above and beyond that reality, a non-physical, spiritual but conscious entity, then you will see this physical reality as unreal, or a secondary reality. You will see how easy it is to give the material world the status of the 'only' reality. And you will start to see that it's just a mirage of passing objects, scenes and images. You realize and remember what you already know, which is that all *events, scenes* and *things* come to pass, and pass they do.

In this lower material reality nothing ever stays the same. Everything is changing. But in the reality of your consciousness, which is you, you are aware that YOU are the one constant. The 'real' you never changes. You realize and remember that 'in that reality' you cannot hold on to anything or anyone. The hand of your body can grasp a chair, but YOU, cannot. You are not your hand just as you are not the hammer in your hand.

When you believe this material reality is the only reality, then you seek love in life in the world outside you. You seek your peace in life, your happiness in life, in the world. And as you now know, when you do seem to find and feel what seems like peace, or what seems to be happiness, in this material world, neither lasts. They fade into nothing, because it was not real, it was just a passing scene, a temporary stimulation, a fleeting sensation, a temporary agitation. As you also now know, in theory at least, if you enter into your own consciousness, into your 'inner space', without grasping anything, without attaching to any idea, image or memory, you will find an enduring source of peace and a pure and natural intention to give of your self and to connect with others, which is love.

An unshakable contentment is always present when you are fully present in and to your self. Being present means free of anger (the past) and free of fear (about the future). When fully present, you will perceive and feel the reality of the 'presence of contentment'. This will begin to dissolve your need for physical stimulations, and that in turn will dissolve your urge to posses, thereby weakening your habit of attaching. Then your emotional habits of creating sadness, anger and fear will fade.

As soon as you see and fully realize, that you cannot possess anything, you also know that you cannot lose anything. Loss will be impossible. Sadness will be impossible. You will have broken the cycle. You are then free. And you cannot be happy unless you are free. Ultimately this redefines and repositions freedom, which is not just the ability to fly anywhere you like, buy or eat anything you like or say whatever you like wherever and whenever you want. True freedom is an inner state of being where there is no longer any attachment, craving or dependency. Sadness, anger and fear are no more. With that freedom there comes an inner state of contentment, and sense of responsibility that extends to assist others to be free within themselves.

Sympathy and Empathy

Sympathy is not empathy, but it's one of the most common confusions in the arena of emotional intelligence. Sympathy is feeling sorry for someone. It is to create sorrow in oneself in response to the perceived plight of another. It's just another of ego's games as the self 'identifies' with the situation and the emotions of the other and thereby creates the same emotional pain. To empathize, on the other hand, is to be sensitive to the feelings of the other (the emotions they are creating and feeling) without creating the same emotions within ones self. Many of us have learned to believe that we have to be in the same emotional state as the other in order to understand and help the other through their emotional turmoil. But this is more non-sense, more myth, once again sustained to a large extent by our entertainment industry. It's like saying you need to be drunk to know someone else is drunk. In fact, it's like saying you need to be drunk to help someone out of their drunkenness. Have you ever seen two drunks trying to help each other? Only when there is the absence of all emotion within your self can you be open, clear and sensitive enough to 'sense' the emotions that the other is creating and feeling in themselves. Only then can you extend your self as understanding and as compassion. Only then can you give authentic care to the other. And both compassion and care are love in action. You cannot empathise with another if you yourself are emotionally disturbed.

Making Love Real

So now you know the difference between emotions and feelings! You know that love is not sourced outside your self. You know that whatever you do, give, or even receive, with love, then you feel that love first 'on the way out'. But how do you 'do love', how do you make love real, and therefore feel 'real love'? This brings us into the territory of your values.

In a simple exercise, during courses and retreats on emotional and spiritual intelligence, I will ask the group to write down what they value most in life. Take a moment and make a list for yourself. 'Value' means what you *care about most* in your life.

Most groups usually co-create a list similar to the following:

Your Values (what you care about most)

Home	Family	Health	Trust
Integrity	Peace	Freedom	Joy
Respect	Honesty	Happiness	Dog
Love	Contentment	Friends	Compassion

If you did your own list on a separate piece of paper, add any of the above that are missing. Then take a moment to contemplate and decide which one is your 'deepest value'. What do you care about most? Most people usually select one of three - Family, Friends or Health.

However the answer is the same for us all, everywhere and at all times. Why do you/we go to work? Because you need to exchange your energy for money? Why do you need the money? To put food on the table, a roof on the house and petrol in the car. But why do you want the bigger house, or the better holiday or the nicer car? Because you 'believe' that when you get these things you will be HAPPY.

Everything every human being does is motivated by the search for happiness, even when they know it may only be temporary. In fact, every human being is motivated by three things during their entire life. At all times, your search for these three things (which of course are not things) motivates what you do. You seek **love** in your relationships, **peace** in your heart and **happiness** in your life. Why do you want a nice **family** and good **friends**? Because then there will be lots of **love,** and you will be **happy**? Why do you want good **health**? Because then you will be at **peace** within yourself, and therefore **happy**? Why does the worst criminal want his enemy 'out of the way'? Because he believes he will then be happy. It's obviously not the right kind of happiness! But it is still the motive.

Regardless of what you are doing, where you are going, what you are wanting, you are always seeking love, peace and happiness in some way or other? Next question – what do these three 'core values' have in common? They have four things in common beginning with the letters IN. They are INternal, INvisible, INtangible and INaudible. In other words they are 'non-physical'. You cannot cut them, eat them, burn them, drown them, touch them or see them. So where are they? They are within you, within the 'I' that says 'I am'. They are within each one of us. You can prove it to you. At least once a year you will buy a gift for a friend or parent. As you give that gift you will say, "This is from me to you with LOVE." Where was that love? In the department store? In the gift? In the wrapping? No! It came from within YOU. That means it was already there. It means it can never not be there. So why do you spend your entire life going 'out there', outside your self, for what you already have within you? It is the paradox of our modern age.

What we seek is already within us. But perhaps you're thinking, "Wait a minute, let's do a reality check here. If love, peace and happiness are already and always within me, why am I not feeling them all the time?" Perhaps that's because you have been taught to 'believe' that, to feel those things, you have to go and get something or be something, or find someone. But the truth is that the only way to feel those things is to go and 'give' something, because when you give the gift with love, who feels that love first, on the way out? You do! Now don't get me wrong here. I am not saying you should go back into the office tomorrow and start going round saying, "I Love You," to everyone. Well you can if you want, but I probably wouldn't recommend it. (if you do, let me know how it goes!) But what does the energy of love look like in action? What are the behaviours that are motivated, shaped and driven by love. Take a moment to list on a piece of paper, and you will likely come up with a list something like this.

Co-operation
Compassionate   Nurtures
Acceptance   Cares
Acknowledges   Gives
Respects   Appreciates
Empathises   **LOVE**   Understands
              in Action
Encourages   Sacrifices
Supports   Shares
Kind   Forgives
Empowers   Helps

Think about your workplace for a moment. Just for a moment, take away the policies and procedures, rules and regulations, products and services, and what are you left with? People. Relationships. In fact you don't go to work every day, you go into a community of relationships. You go and interact with a bunch of people. So as you go into work you can sense Henry is down. And you know why, because Henry told you yesterday that he lost someone in his family. So you *empathise* and *support* him through his sadness. You shape the very energy of your self into empathy and you sit down and listen to Henry, and then support him till he gets through his downer. Whereas Hilary has just had a run-in with the boss and she is feeling rejected. So how do you respond to Hilary? You *encourage* her and *empower* her to restore her self esteem. Madge on the other hand is confused. She can't get clear about some ideas she is working on. So with Madge, you sit and give some time, and *co-operate* and *help* her to *create* and *clarify* her ideas.

So as you go into work and encounter the people you work with, you are sensing what they are feeling (usually their emotional state), and therefore what they 'need'. Then, using the energy (love) that you already have within you, the energy that you are, you meet that need. And when you do, who feels it first on the way out? You do. They may say 'thank you'. It's not that you want or need them to say a 'thank you', but if they do you accept their gratitude and in that moment you affirm your own value. If it doesn't come it's OK, as you are no longer needy for something you already have.

So now take blank page, draw two lines from top to bottom so that there are three columns. In the first column write down the names of five people that you work with every day. Anyone will do. In the second column, identify the value that is appropriate to meet what you perceive is the need of that person. And in the third column visualise and describe the behaviour that will deliver that value to that person.

The Core Value is Love (see diagram on previous page) which is YOU, and then all the secondary values that emerge from love, are what you see around it. These are some of the many faces and forms that you are able to give to what you are. The third column is your behaviour, as you express or deliver that value, as you embody that value. What would you be doing, what would your 'delivery' of that value look like if someone was watching you? For example:

David
Is struggling to get a report done by the Friday deadline.
So the **value** here is **support.**
And the **behaviour** is: Tomorrow at lunchtime I will take 45 minutes and do the 'difficult statistics' for David.

Mary
Is depressed.
So the **value** is **empathy.**
And the **behaviour** is: Tomorrow morning at 9am I'll take Mary out for a coffee and just listen to her story in order to understand why she is depressed and, in doing so, it may help her to navigate her way out of her emotional state.

At this point you may say, "Well why should I be the one who always gives, gives, gives?" Surely they have to give something in return. Surely they will just take advantage of me if I am the one who is always giving. And besides, it's tiring."

You are acting from what is true in you, from the energy of your heart. You are using the energy of your heart, which is love, and as you use it, give it, in whatever form, you are the first to feel it and be empowered by it. It won't work a) if you are giving with any resentment or b) if you want something in return. Seeking a return is what kills your power and in fact you are not really giving, you are taking, because you are expecting. And that's why it can feel tiring. As soon as you want something back for your self then your energy is stuck and not flowing, and that's what makes you tired, not the fact that you are always giving and they are always taking. It's your thoughts of subtle judgment and resentment when your expectations are not met that are tiring you, draining you. Then you blame 'them' and compound the matter by creating more resentment. You have forgotten that only the ego expects. Love has no expectations. Only the ego blames and resents. Love always accepts the other as they are, even if they refuse to accept your care, that's fine, it's their choice. But a refusal of love as care, as empathy, as help, today, is likely to turn into to acceptance tomorrow. Which is why it has been said that 'infinite patience creates instant results!'

When you are free of wanting something in return, when you are not busy with expectations of the other, then if they do try to take advantage of your generosity you will sense it, but not resent it. All you need to do is be a little assertive and sense when enough is enough, so that you don't allow them to become dependent on you. This kind of sensitivity only comes with experience, as well as your own freedom from being dependent on them being dependent on you!

So there you have it. You have a clear choice. You can live from your learned **beliefs** or from your innate **values**. You can allow your thoughts, attitudes and behaviours to be shaped by your assimilated belief systems, or you can access what you value most, which is already at the heart of your heart, and allow that to shape how you respond to others in particular, and to life in general. It's a clear choice that seems to be no choice when the ego is at work. It will become an unnecessary choice when your values make a long awaited return to your daily life.

Beyond Your Beliefs

It sounds easy but the attachment to those beliefs is deep. Your ego has 'dug into' your subconscious. Attachment to many of those beliefs is simply outside your day-to-day and moment-to-moment awareness. Your ego will strongly resist your attempts to go 'beyond belief' and access your values. One sign of that resistance is the thought, "But I can't just go round being selflessly loving towards everyone, that's cloud cuckoo land stuff!"

It takes the inner work of 'attention' and 'awareness' to see the beliefs you are using to sabotage your self. As you do you will also start to see how you use your beliefs to block your values, and that will help you to recognize how others are using their beliefs to sabotage their values. If, for example, you have learned to **believe** that competition is good and necessary, it will sabotage your value and ability to give co-operation. It means that you have not yet realized that competition generates fear, whereas co-operation is an expression of love. Competition is ego driven and therefore against the nature of the authentic self. If you **believe** that anger is OK and sometimes useful you will notice it sabotages your value and ability to give empathy towards another – you cannot empathise with others if you are angry at their mistakes.

If you **believe** that life is basically survival of the fittest, then that **belief** will sabotage your 'value of giving' and your ability to serve others. When the chips are down, you will serve your own needs before you serve others. Only when you start to see how your beliefs suppress your values, can you consciously correct them, let go of them, eliminate them or change them. Or you can go straight to the heart of your self where you will always find the power of the energy we call love, and you can start clearing a pathway through the jungle of your beliefs and out into the world of your behaviours. And as love finds its way out as care, compassion and co-operation, the hundreds of learned beliefs, like 'me first', 'they are wrong' and 'life is only for winners and losers', will simply begin to atrophy.

Once again, some form of meditation and self reflection is necessary. Only then will you begin to see the truth about all beliefs which, as we saw earlier, ironically lies within the word 'belief' itself. BeLIEfs are lies. Beliefs are what we create and attach to when we lose awareness of what is true. As you realise that beliefs are essentially illusions, they fall away to reveal an innate sense of what is true. You already know what is true. It's simply an assimilated belief system that is getting in the way.

This is why even 'self-belief' doesn't really help in the long run. Yes it seems to give you a spurt of confidence power. It can seem to inject you with a burst of achievement power. But in the long term it's draining, and the doubt that must exist underneath the attachment to any self-belief will get a chance to surface. (if it doesn't it's likely to quietly tear you apart inside). Much better to know and allow the power of truth to be the foundation of your life. When you KNOW what you are, which is a source of peace, a source of love, of pure joy, then you don't need to believe it. You don't need to seek these states, or achieve these states. You don't need to impose, or force a belief system about your self upon your self. You don't need to attach your self to a belief based image of yourself, which of course just becomes another form of ego. When you 'know' the truth about you, and you live that truth, self-belief is no longer necessary. Then you don't need to waste future time and energy affirming and sustaining a set of beliefs about your self. 'Belief power' is a weak power next to the power of truth.

But we do assimilate and cling on to many beliefs. And we don't realise how disempowering they can be in our daily life. That means we don't challenge our belief systems very often. Let's do a couple of examples. Perhaps three of the most common beliefs today are at the core of our culture. They can be found in almost all societies. But they are not true.

Commonly Held Belief 1 - Real happiness can be purchased

To most people, it's obviously not true. Happiness derived from any purchase always fades, leaving a craving for more. And craving is not happiness, it's discontentment. Yet even when we seem to know this, we still act as if we need to buy our happiness. So strong and deeply rooted is this belief, we become completely blind to the reality that our craving, desiring, wanting the next purchase are all symptoms of unhappiness.

Commonly Held Belief 2 - Success is achievement

To many people this belief is still a truth, but to an increasing number it's an obvious illusion. It's a belief that keeps us trapped in a process of struggling and striving, always looking to the future for an accomplishment and therefore always dissatisfied now. Success is not struggling or dissatisfaction. It's more likely to be the ability to be content within oneself in the moment, in every moment, yet still do the right thing, in the right way with the right intention.

Commonly Held Belief 3 - Others make you feel what you feel

Yes here it is again. But it's an illusion, and until you fully recognize that it's an illusion, you will see your self as a perpetual victim and never realize the truth that you make you feel what you feel and that you have the power to choose your feelings, in all situations at all times'. Now that's an empowering truth. But remember, don't believe me. See for your self.

These beliefs are fairly easy to identify as false, but the attachment to (and identification with) them is so deep that the ego will fight when you attempt to let them go and live a different way, a truer way. In fact when you make this kind of effort within yourself, it can feel like you are dying a little. And the ego will find clever ways to hold on, to stay alive. It will throw up thoughts like, "Well I'm not sure, maybe some competition is OK…maybe security is totally dependent on money…well it's only human to get angry!"

As we saw earlier, the most prevalent belief that we all define ourselves by is 'I am this body'. To release this one belief alone can feel a little like dying alive. The belief that 'I am the form that I occupy' gives rise to the belief that death is inevitable. It's the belief that we hold on to most and around which we generate the most fear. But do you die? Will you come to an end. The majority would likely say 'yes of course'. A small minority say only the body dies, but the self, as the soul or spirit, lives on. Others say it is impossible to know. And then there are those who say they do know that they won't die, as they have had some 'insperience' of their immortality, their infinity, their eternity. In the absence of such an 'insperience' perhaps the truest stance is to say, "I don't know." No one can prove it's true, but equally no one can prove there is no existence of the self after the end of the body.

What you do know from your own experience however, is that everything comes and goes. Nothing stays. And what you do know is that when you hold on to anything that comes to you and you don't let go, it makes life miserable. Perhaps misery is too strong a word. Perhaps discomfort is the beginning. Then insecurity. Then stress. This is why attachment is at the root of all suffering. And when you are attached and suffering it just means you are not being your true self, which really means you are not living a true life. When you attach to anything, it's as if you are slowly suffocating your self with…your attachments. And as you do, the stress of holding on and fearing loss gradually increases. It's as if you are killing your self as you live, and you therefore miss your life. Which is why 'dying alive', which just means consciously letting go of all you are holding on to, is the way to live... truely! And when you do let go of all that you are attached to, and identified with, only then can you 'be' your self.

Only then can the true you be revealed, only then is true love revealed, because all fear is gone. All the attachments, that you have used to surround and suppress the light of your heart, are gone. Only then are you truly free. Only then can you give without condition. And only then can you be authentically happy. It all sounds neat and easy in words but of course the reality of implementation in day-to-day life is something else. Which is why some time each day in some process of contemplation or meditation is necessary.

But How Long Will It Take?

As you may have recognised, the shift from ego (misidentification) to an awareness of the authentic self, the shift from attachment to non-attachment, from 'emotional' reactions to 'feeling' responses, from beliefs to values, are all part of what has been called the 'spiritual journey'.

This 'journey' idea is simply a neat way of describing a process of realization or awakening. In reality it is a journey that doesn't go anywhere! You are already there. You cannot be anywhere else but 'at home' in your heart. And the heart of you is you. In reality you have never been away. It only seemed so. And what 'seems so' is not real, just something that passes. Everything you have seen, everything you have felt and everything that you thought you knew or have known, on this apparent journey... passes.

So that old saying is almost literally true, 'everything comes to pass'! Against the permanent reality of you, everything else is temporary and therefore unreal, or if you prefer, less 'real'. You only make one recurring mistake and that is to attempt to make the unreal real, you attempt to make the less real as real as you, you attempt to halt the flow and stop what must pass from passing! And in so doing you keep losing your self 'in' the unreal. Yes the car is there, it is sitting out on the road, and you do drive it. But the car, like every 'thing' else will pass. It's real, but not as real as you. But when you attach to and identify with it, you are losing your self in a lesser reality, a mental reality, as the car is just an image in your mind. And that will cause you to suffer. If you are OK with suffering then of course that is your choice. But notice, that you start to believe, that one of the ways to alleviate your sufferingis by acquiring a bigger, shinier, newer version of the car! And so the downward spiral from the reality of who you 'really are' down into what you are really not, continues.

In the Beginning

Very often the questions arises as to how this spiral began. How did spirit, the self, start to lose itself in the material, in the world, in the first place. Without proceeding to write another book, this is how it may have happened, in one paragraph! See if you can remember and recognise the process for your self. See if you can intuit the process.

It began as the play of innocence when your innocence knew nothing other than pure play. Like a child, you new nothing about life, so all you did was joyfully play. And as you and I played together we co-created... a 'play'. And as we grew together we both began to give the status of 'reality' to our creation and gradually it seemed to become more real than we were as the creators. Until one day we allowed ourselves to be overcome by 'the play' and we lost our self 'in' the play. And innocence was no more. Seriousness replaced our playfulness and, as we attached to and identified with our co-created play, and to things in the play, including memories of how yesterdays playfulness was so good and much better than today, we gave birth to the ego and we created fear, which is, in truth, miscreation.

At any moment you can collapse all that and see for your self that all around you is still just play. A play of light and energy, that is never still, and never real, at least never as real against the reality of you, the one who is seeing, watching, witnessing ...the play. And the moment you see, the moment you realize you are the one who is watching, the one who is unchanging, the one who knows not the passing of time, knows not the sorrow of loss, knows not the fear of suffering or the suffering that is fear, you are home again.

It is the journey of one second and no distance. Words cannot take you where you already and always are. But if they could they might read and sound like this.

Sit quietly
Just watch
Observe everything
Be still
Stay silent
See who is seeing
You are the one that cannot be observed
Cannot be seen
And yet you see
You are the seer
Invisible to your self
Notice… 'I am witness' to all except my self
And know only I is real
All else rises and falls, ebbs and flows, emerges and fades
Until even the 'I' becomes unreal
An idea that also fades
And everything is
And you are
Here

Now I think I can hear you thinking, "But what about the electricity bill, what about the company's share price, what about the kids dinner, what about the state of the world , what about the war in…"

It's all play! It's simply a play of light and sound, movement and change, ebbing and flowing, rising and falling. If you stop and simply watch for a moment, any scene in the play, local or global, at home or abroad, you will see emotion coming through to shape every scene. This is what creates drama. Now you know that all emotion comes from the ego, which is the self identifying with what is not the self, and is therefore unreal, an illusion. So what you are watching 'out there' is a scene playing out in front of you, but it's based on unreality, on an illusion. It appears to be real, but it's made up mostly of unreality i.e. the ego and emotions of others. But it's OK, as that is exactly what is meant to happen, and as soon as you see it for what it is, and realize it's OK, it's just a play, your home. You are home in the reality of you. It's just that you keep wanting to leave home, go 'out there' and interfere with the play, fix the scene, punish the characters, make your mark, be recognized, feel wanted, get approval...from within 'the play'. And so your ego comes alive again.

It's not that you just sit watching, doing nothing, being passive. The art of life as awaiting the invitation to participate. You will always get an invitation to participate. And then you make a contribution to the play according to that invitation. And if you are free of ego. If you are at peace, if you are open, if you are detached, then there will be no emotion, just the light of your love, of you, flowing from you into whatever 'scene' you are participating in. This is to be a co-creator. And depending on the 'quality' of your contribution so will be the frequency of future invitations.

That's why you will almost always hold within your awareness a subtle question, "Is my contribution from my ego, or is it coming from the authentic self, the real me, the true I?" When you think and act from ego you only sustain the illusion that 'the play', that life, is a serious business, a serious matter, and therefore add more fear, anger and sadness to the play. When you think and act from the true you then you bring love, light and power to the play. This in turn helps others to see through the illusions within the play, to free themselves from the beliefs that sustain their habit of 'attaching' and therefore their misery and their stress.

Only then is happiness possible.

Part THREE

A
HAPPY
Story

A story of a future past.
But don't forget, it's just a story!

Once upon a time,
in the not too distant future…

You wake up one morning and much like every other morning, you drag your self half-heartedly out of bed and into the bathroom. A quick glance in the mirror is enough to shock your self fully awake! Sometimes the most pleasurable part of the day is that ten minutes in the shower, as you struggle mentally with the acceptance of 'here we go again, another day, another dollar'.

After enrobing your body with something 'safe', the next destination is the kitchen, as you surrender to the recurring feeling that you are stuck in your own version of groundhog day. Just like most other days, you move around the kitchen like a ballroom dancer! You shuffle to kettle, shimmy to the toaster, quick step to the sink, pirouette to the fridge, foxtrot back to the toaster and glide over to the table. Time for a rest already. And as your eyes stare straight through the wall, your hand brings toast to mouth to confirm 'the program' is still working.

Then it hits you like a ton of muesli. You've been 'had'. You've fallen for the biggest ruse, the greatest cosmic joke of all time. You've been sold a thousand pigs in a poke. In one single atom-splitting moment, you realize that every single promise you have ever been made has been broken. Why? Because every single promise was targeted at the same outcome, which was your happiness. And no-one has the right to promise happiness to another. It's impossible. It can never be delivered. Suddenly you've got it, by jove you've got it! Every single promise could never be kept. But you believed. Boy, did you believe. NOW you know why your life was, and is, increasingly cratered with moments of misery. NOW you know why you really do live with a quiet desperation which you have brilliantly learned to disguise. NOW you know why happiness is so damned elusive.

As you look around the kitchen, it now seems as if every item, every object, is screaming at you to WAKE UP. Not from another restless night in bed, but from the dream that your life has become. Every object suddenly takes on a whole new symbolic meaning. The oven, that multi-tasking item, around which the kitchen is built, represents the promise they made that, when you get a good job, a good position in life, do your many tasks well, receive lots of recognition, when you 'cook up' a good career, then you will be happy. They promised that if you study hard and got 'that position,' then you will have 'arrived' and you will be happy. When your career is fully baked in the oven or your life only then can you rest contentedly on your laurels. But instead of making you happy the job, like the oven, is just a place of heat and pressure. A claustrophobic container with a tiny window to look out of when you get bored. It was a false promise because now you know work can never generate real and lasting happiness. It's 'work' for God's sake! And when did work ever make anyone…happy?

The kettle is the best money can buy. It's a prestige kettle – even its brand name is Prestige. 'They' promised that when others recognize you by your achievements, when others uphold and celebrate your reputation, you will have attained the 'prestige', the recognition, 'they' said everyone craves, that will bring you happiness. But now you know it doesn't bring happiness, it just brings the insecurity that comes with dependence on others for your self esteem and self respect. It only generates worry thoughts about what others think about you. And that's not happiness, that's…worry.

There in front of you, on the table you've sat at for the last ten years, is the toaster, the fastest little elemental cooker. Now it just reminds you that 'they' said that, if you work harder and faster, then, and only then, you will deserve to be happy. So you worked harder, with a dedication that sometimes bordered on obsessive, and how did you feel? Like a piece of flaming toast. Burnt out.

And today, just like every other day, strewn around the worktop next to the toaster is 'stuff'. Useless objects that shouldn't even be in the kitchen. But they promised that when you have all the right stuff in life, the shiny car, the platinum credit card, the best sofa, curtains, bed, carpet, shoes, all the 'quality' stuff, then you would be happy. But you're not happy. In fact the more stuff that arrives just means more space is filled with things that do almost nothing and mean nothing. Just looking at all the stuff is exhausting. And 'they' said 'stuff' should be your measure of happiness.

Even the place mat on the table has a picture of the perfect mansion house, in the romantic country village, with horses passing the front gate, implying that you too can live and find contentment in the last tranquil corner of the world. 'They' promised, when you make such an image real in your life, which in fact you did many years ago, you will be happiest of the happy. But you aren't, you're just bored. Any romance around the perfectly ideal location wore off on week three when the weeds outgrew the flowers.

And just as you are feeling lighter for your intellectual realizations, there, sitting in the middle of the kitchen table, is the ever present centerpiece, the perfectly paired, gold plated, salt and pepper shakers. Another great big false promise. 'They' promised that when you find the right person, your soul mate, love at first blush, and you settled down with your partner for life, you will have 'arrived' at the threshold of the highest happiness. But of course it's not like that. It's hard work, it's up and it's down, it's variable according to their moods and your moods. It's sticky sometimes and sweet at others. It's boring sometimes and downright painful at others. It's obvious now that marriage to that perfect partner does not come with happiness built in. But you believed. But now you don't. And it's OK.

Out of the corner of your eye, it's as if the deluxe juicer on the shelf is saying, "Don't forget about me." You remember the day you bought it so that you could lose weight, slim down, get fit and get your body looking good. 'They' promised that if you were sleek and svelte, lean yet lythe, beautiful yet mysterious, then others would like you more, love you more, and you would be happy because they were happy to see how slim and trim you are. So the juicer juiced your new diet and the lean look you craved came true. But you didn't feel any different inside. No wonder, as most people hardly noticed. And all you felt was hungry and irritable and eventually angry. You realize how many unhappy people there must be chasing a prefect physical form after being promised it would bring them happiness. What a waste!

And then there were all those seminars and workshops, all those books and tapes, all in the name of your 'personal development'. That big round salad bowl on the edge of the kitchen sink reminds you of how you did manage to lose some of those 'hard edges' from your character. You did manage to become rounder and softer in your attitude. More embracing of others. They promised you'd be happy if you could achieve all those things and transform your personality. But you're not happier. You're even more torn and tense inside as you try to work out who is the real you and what the real you wants in life. Is it that naughty, edgy, sometimes grumpy old personality that you were quite comfortable with, despite your discomforts. Or is it the so-called new and improved personality with built-in 'cool', custom designed 'tolerance', retro-fitted 'patience', that you are awkwardly trying to develop. Or could you have missed something altogether about this personality development lark?

Either way, whenever you think about self development, it just starts a racket in your head. And you realize personal development is confused with personality and development, and it does not bring about happiness, just various forms of existential confusion.

As you glance up to check the time even the clock, reminds you of 'their' promise that the future is bright. 'They' promised that if you could be more optimistic about life that you would be happy in future times. And now you know. That's nonsense. Standing absolutely still in the middle of your kitchen, looking straight ahead at the clock, the light bulb above your head flickers in resonance with this, your most significant moment of enlightenment so far, as you realize there is no future. It's just a figment of your imagination. A projection of memory imbued with hope and sent flying into a fictional tomorrow with a forced optimism. Happiness is not delivered by the future – it's so obvious now, that there is only *now*. Always, only ever *now*. But they promised. And in that moment, you knew that 'they' didn't know what they were talking about.

Returning to the table, your head shaking slightly at your own incredulity that you actually believed it all, you'd swallowed it all, hook, line and sinker, and as you pick up the knife to butter a piece of toast, the last illusion is shattered. 'They' promised that if you discovered the focus of your life, if you could find the sharpness of a clear purpose for your personal life, only then would be able to see the direction to your life, only then would you be able to cut through all the demands for your time and energy. Only when you follow your unique personal purpose would you be really happy. For a fleeting moment, you recall all those months you agonized over your purpose. What could it be? Is it a special purpose?. Am I special? What will be different when I find it? Where is it? Is it something I have to do? Will it be something only I can do? And as if a huge burden has been lifted from your entire life, you see with pinpoint clarity for the very first time. Life has no purpose other than to live. Life has no purpose other than *living*. All you can do is laugh. Only laugh. And so you laugh.

As you listen to your self laughing, you can detect a mix of laughters. There is the laughter of celebration because now you are free, the laughter of relief from that painful, tense struggle to find happiness has ended. And there is the laughter of having heard the greatest joke ever told. You're laughing, because now you know for sure, that living happily has nothing to do with what has happened or what might happen, it has nothing to do with what you have achieved or what you have accumulated. 'Living happiness' is what you are. Toast never tasted so good.

The 13 Myths About Happiness

It is the holy grail of daily living and a satisfying life. Its acquisition motivates almost everything we do. Perhaps no other subject has generated so many books, gurus and seminars. It is happiness.

Not the temporary happiness of a good night out or a good long holiday, or even a good long relationship. But real happiness, that is probably not best described by the word 'happiness'. which tends to indicate a 'high state' in contrast to a 'low state'.

Real happiness is neither high nor low. It's not acquired or accumulated. And it's not dependent on anything or found anywhere. It can't be earned or stored. And it's certainly cannot be manufactured and packaged.

Before we explore the what, where and how of authentic happiness, let's clear away the myths that get in the way. Once again we encounter a mythology, an evolved and disturbing set of false beliefs, about something that is so fundamental to the human spirit that you are.

Myth 1

Happiness is Measured by Your Purchasing Power

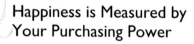

It's not difficult to dispel this myth. Some of the unhappiest people in the world are the wealthiest in financial terms. And some of the happiest people in the world are living in material poverty. Wander through almost any Indian village, look at the bright sparkling eyes and happy smiles of many, if not most, children and you see a vision of happiness. They have almost no money and no material possessions and live on one bowl of rice a day.

Myth 2

Happiness is Dependent on How Much You Can Accumulate

Believe this and your mind will likely sound like an old record with the needle stuck in the same groove and the only song that emerges is Money Money Money or More More More. The more you have the more you want, and the more you worry about what you think you have, the more you worry that you might not get even more, and the more you worry about losing what you have not yet got. And this is happiness?

Myth 3

Happiness has to be Earned

Yes it's that Scottish Protestant work ethic that says that the only path to happiness is through the guilt that you're not working hard enough. This means that you are carrying a belief that you have to deserve to be happy, that you cannot be happy until you have worked hard enough to the satisfaction of others. And you can never work hard enough, so you will never be happy. You can never satisfy others, because now you know everyone decides their own satisfactions. You can never be happy as long as you believe it has to be earned. All you will likely feel is guilty.

Myth 4

Happiness is the Achievement of your Dreams and Desires.

Dare to dream .... they say! If you can dream it, you can achieve it... they say! You have to know what you want and want it bad enough... they say! But what they don't say is that desiring is craving, and that any satisfaction from the achievement of any desire/craving can only ever be temporary before a new desire/craving knocks on the door. Sometimes it's called addiction, and happiness is not the satisfaction of an addiction. How do you know? Watch for the fear that sits at the heart of all desire, and watch for the emptiness that sits and grows at the centre of the temporary satisfaction at the fulfilment of any desire.

Myth 5

Happiness is Always in the Future

Otherwise known as 'delay'. It is the language of, "I'll be happy... when we get married...when we have a family... when the kids have left home... when we retire..." It becomes a habit to see happiness always tomorrow and seldom today, seldom now. Until there is the realization that there is only today, only now, true happiness will always be as elusive as an oasis in the desert is to someone dying of thirst. You may think you see it up ahead, shimmering in the distance, you may believe you are making your way towards it, but you never arrive.

Myth 6

Happiness is only Possible when Everything is just Perfect

If you are a perfectionist it is likely that you will experience much day-to-day stress and tension. It is an imperfect world where nothing can ever be perfect. Why? Because perfection is personal. For a perfectionist even perfection is imperfect. Simply because perceiving imperfection is to project your own imperfection. But don't tell that to a perfectionist as they are unlikely to see it that way. Somewhere and from someone (usually a parent) they learned that only by doing something perfectly (to someone else's standards) could they be perfect. A classic mistake. In this chaotic world nothing can ever be perfect. Only when the perfectionist accepts everything as it is, can they find contentment. That's because everything is perfect just as it is. Not 'perfect' perfect, but just as it is, because that's how everything is meant to be. As it is.

Myth 7

Happiness is Dependent on Others

Perhaps the most prevalent illusion is the one we touched on earlier, that others are responsible for your happiness. From this comes the victim mindset and a perpetual unhappiness that most of us eventually settle for. In effect we become happy being unhappy and the world affirms this by saying, "Well done, you are now a member of the Normal Club because normal people are frequently unhappy. In the meantime keep searching for that greater, ultimate happiness. And by the way, we have a nice little advert here that you might like to watch..." Having said that, it is obvious that our society is dependent on us all continuing to outsource our happiness. To end our dependency on 'the external' to stimulate our feelings of happiness in 'the internal' would be a revolutionary shift in both consciousness and behaviour. Right now we are all 'materially dependent' on others living the myth that happiness is a dependency!

Myth 8

Happiness is Control

The natural extension of dependency, and probably the ego's favourite impulse and intention, is to attempt to control what can never be controlled. Occasionally, when someone does do what you want, it appears that you controlled them, and of course there is a kind of happiness to be had from that. But it's just another illusion – a double illusion actually. You didn't control them because it's impossible to control another human being. And the high of happiness, that little kick that comes with the illusion of your power over others, subsides fast and off you go in search of your next opportunity to try to make the world dance to your tune. In between? Only frustration and anger, and an unhappy life spent mostly in resistance, as the world and people in the world, fail to do exactly what you want.

Myth 9

Happiness is just a Feeling

Of course you can 'feel' happy, but happiness is not just a feeling. Feelings pass. Happiness, as we shall see, is a state that can take various inner forms, and each state can be felt. But happiness is not just a feeling.

Myth 10

Happiness is Receiving Recognition

Attempting to please others is a pernicious habit that can rule and ruin whole lifetimes. Usually learned at our mother and father's knee, and then from our teachers, we come to believe we are not worthy unless and until we are recognized by others, until others are happy with us. People-pleasing becomes a thread that runs through our work and family life. But it comes with the background tension that we may fail to please and therefore lose out on receiving recognition and approval. What could be a happy life turns into continuous anxiety that we may not gain or that we may lose the approval of others. And eventually resentment will arise as we come to believe we are being ignored, that we are being denied the recognition we believe we deserve. Or we give up trying and hopelessness and helplessness take over.

Myth 11

Happiness is Winning

Winning is only a 'high' when you believe you have to compete your way through life, when you believe the cliché 'you are either a winner or a loser'. But even in a competitive context you cannot win all the time. You can't be 'high' on winning all the time, there will have to be lows if you indulge in the highs. You will eventually find that the occasional high that comes with winning, becomes more occasional. Just as using drugs to get high becomes addictive, so the high of winning can be addictive. But you cannot stay high, so an increasing amount of drug to stay high rather than low is required, so the addict becomes less and less 'high happy'.

Shooting up on winning all the time will eventually have the same effect as being on drugs all the time – which is no effect at all. Winning is not a way to happiness because life is not meant to be competitive. There are no winners and losers in 'reality'. Just those who believe they are winners and losers. Competition is ego's game designed to keep us busy believing in the dualistic doctrine of inferior and superior.

Myth 12

Happiness is Sensual and Sensation

When you believe you are only a physical being you start to believe you can only become happy through some sensual stimulation.

Eventually neediness grows for greater and greater sensation to deliver the stimulated high that you associate with 'happiness'. This is the primary illusion that almost runs the world. It only collapses when you know your self as you are, and when you realize your physical body is only your dwelling place and that your senses are not the source of your happiness. Besides, how could you ever be happy spending your life watching your self decay? Freedom from this trap is only possible when there is self realization. Not exactly the first lesson in primary school.

Myth 13

Happiness is Dependent on Others' Happiness

What difference would it make to your life and your relationships if you discovered that you don't 'have to' make others happy because you can't make others happy. 'Others' means anyone and everyone. It's the other side of the 'others make me happy' coin. In truth you cannot make someone happy, only they can do that. Truly realizing this can be healing, as most childhoods were spent being on the receiving end of our parents attempts to emotionally blackmail us. They would say, "If you are a good boy/girl, mummy will be happy and then you can be happy." Which is mummy really saying, "My happiness is dependent on you." It's not long until we blindly believe we cannot be happy unless others are happy. Hence the reason some people spend their life trying to make others happy. They may never know that it's impossible.

Why so many illusions surrounding happiness?
A) Each myth does deliver a little of what we have come to call happiness, but it's just a short buzz, a temporary high, it's not authentic happiness.
B) Each one is based on the deepest fallacy, that happiness comes from outside in.
C) No one teaches us otherwise in a formal sense, largely because the true way to human happiness threatens the foundations

upon which our societies exist. Countries and governments, and therefore banks and businesses, all exist because they sit on a foundation that could be called the 'mythology of happiness'.

The True Meaning of Happiness

So what then is the way to true happiness? Is there a way, a route, a journey, or is that just another myth. The answer lies first in the understanding of the true meaning of happiness. In a sense happiness is the wrong word as it tends to infer a kind of 'excited gleefulness'. But as we have seen, excitement is not happiness, it's excitement, it's agitation. However, like love, happiness takes various forms. Although we can name each form the realization of each requires a certain understanding and practice. The three main forms of authentic happiness are best described as contentment, joy and bliss.

In this dualistic world our language is designed to identify, describe and acknowledge opposites. And so we make the mistake of describing inner states of being in terms of opposites. As fear is sometimes seen as the opposite of love in a dualistic sense, so sadness is seen as the opposite of happiness. But in truth (which is that which never changes), in reality (and the highest reality is only that which is within you – which is you), love has no opposite and happiness has no opposite, because opposites do not exist within consciousness, within the self. Consciousness is ONE, the self is ONE. So while describing the three states of happiness, it's not that they exist as 'separate' inner states. They are simply potential vibrations of you or states of your consciousness.

Your mission, should you decide to accept it, is to regain control over your self from the ego. It is to restore self-mastery so that the quality of your consciousness, the level of the vibration of your consciousness, of your state of being, is fully under your command. In so doing you will restore your ability to be constantly and authentically happy everywhere and at all times. Well that's the possibility! Here is how.

Authentic Happiness is Undisturbable CONTENTMENT

Contentment is the result of the inner work of self-realisation. Contentment is only possible when you know who and what you are. And that is only possible when you realize you can never be, and never were, anything or anyone else. Sounds simple until you realize you have spent your entire life either thinking you were, or trying to be, something or someone else! That's ego's game as we have already seen – either defending and protecting a false sense of self (no contentment in that) or striving and struggling to attain a false sense of self (no contentment in that). But once all that ends and there is the genuine sense of 'I am', then all those roles at work and at home, and everywhere else in life, become just that, roles that you play. So life becomes what it really is…playful or full of play.

Contentment is only possible when you arrive at the awareness that everything near and far, in the world around you, is exactly the way it is meant to be in this moment now and that there is only this moment now. Not so easy when you realize you have spent your entire life avoiding being fully present in this moment now. Avoiding the present is the ego's way of killing your contentment.

Contentment is only possible when you are able to accept everyone as they are at every moment in every situation. That means an end to judging or resisting others, an end to complaining and blaming, an end to trying to change others and world events. Not so easy after a lifetime of armchair judgment, resistance and rejection. It does not mean just sitting back and doing nothing. It means the re-awakening of self-responsibility and seeing that self-responsibility is inextricably linked to world responsibility. In other words, it is only when you cease to project what you think and feel onto others and create actions aligned with what is true within you, that you can make the most effective contribution to the world.

When others are seen to be NOT acting in alignment with what is true in them, your response is not one of judgment and condemnation (which kills your contentment), but one of compassion and understanding (which maintains your contentment). These are acts of love which bring the light and energy of love into the world. There is an understanding that all violence at all levels is the ego at work. It is human beings making a mistake about who they are, and that mistake can be corrected. But this can only be by demonstration, not by force, only through influence, not control.

This way to the form of happiness that is contentment, can be seen by some as passive and a form of avoidance. But in truth it takes great courage to show others the 'power' of this way (acceptance), when all around are attempting to use the 'force' of the ego (resistance). Force is simply a form of attempted control and you cannot force anyone to correct their misidentification, you cannot force anyone to detach themselves from an image in their own mind with which they are mistakenly identifying themselves.

Being contened is not doing nothing. It is the foundation for seeing clearly and creating the most accurate and appropriate way forward.

Authentic Happiness as Unbridled JOY

Joy is only possible when your life energy (you) flows out into the world, free of the desire for any part of the world to flow towards you. As a creative being, your deepest joy is when you are being creative and when your creativity is aligned with the truth 'in' you, the truth 'of' you. Not the limited creativity of painting and poetry, but the creation of your life.

That means realizing that you are designed to give of yourself whole-heartedly at every moment. Not so easy when you realize how half-heartedly you have learned to live your life. Half-heartedness happens when you want something for you. Half of your heart (which is you) is focused on bringing something or someone to you, so only half is going out as giving, and probably half of that carries a 'condition' with it. This tension is the 'killjoy' of most lives

In truth, life is not designed to want anything. Life needs nothing, you need nothing. Your body needs food and shelter and clothing, but 'you' need nothing. If there is a need, it is to see and realize the mistakes that you make that give birth to the ego. It is the need to give of your self. Creativity is to give well, to give accurately and generously. Which means to create the most appropriate response to meet the needs of people and the world around you. All of which is only possible when you know your self as love. And when you do, it is joyful or full of joy.

Some may say that to give give give is to be blind to those who would take advantage of your generosity and that it will make you more like a joyous fool than joyful. But they are stuck in a belief system that says life 'owes' them. They are likely to be someone who still believes they have 'rights'. They have not yet realized that you neither have, nor do you need, rights when you know your responsibilities. Your first responsibility is your ability to respond. Your greatest joy in life will depend on how you use your creative capacity to respond and thereby create your life.

To respond with emotion is to kill one's joy. To respond with love, and the appropriate form or face of love, brings the greatest joy from inside out, not outside in. To respond whole-heartedly means all of your life is flowing one way. It is doing what love is designed to do, extending and connecting, nurturing and nourishing. That is what we are each designed to do. One of the signs of the presence of joy is when the awareness of time passing recedes into the background. You stop looking at the clock. True joy is known beyond the consciousness of time, like the innocent universe of a child at play, before it learns that it has to be home in time for dinner... or else!

Authentic Happiness as Unlimited BLISS

Bliss is only possible when you are completely free. Freedom is only possible when there is no attachment to anything, anyone, any idea, any memory. Birds sing with delight during the bliss of free flight. They are attached to nothing. Nothing is pulling them down. And so it is with the human soul, the self. The lightness of bliss is only possible when you are free of all things that pull you down. And that means no attaching, grasping, holding or protecting anything whatsoever. It also means an end to desiring, which has the object of attachment hidden within it.

Detachment allows the 'fearlessness' that sits at the heart of bliss to emerge within. It is a fearlessness that defies the logic of our beliefs and assumptions in a world in which we are taught to believe is filled with danger. This is probably why so few of us can be heard singing our way through life with consistent delight, because so few are truly free, truly detached, truly without dependency or neediness, truly living in the bliss of free flight!. The ego ensures our imprisonment. And even though our prison is unreal, a temporary construction in consciousness, we spend most of our life building and defending it. Hence most people live their entire life in the absence of the happiness that as bliss.

Being truly free is only possible when you realize that you have spent your life within an illusory or superficial freedom, that is really a prison cell in disguise. The bars of that cell include desire, judgement, resistance and our emotional addictions, each with their roots in attachment to an image that you mistake for your self. Only once the attachment to the image is

Tears of Joy

One question that arises frequently in Emotional Intelligence seminars is around 'tears of joy'. Surely joy is a positive emotion and can be expressed with tears. But true joy would never cry. Tears are a symptom of sadness or a relief from emotional pressure - a form of catharsis. When a new born baby arrives often one or both parents may cry 'tears of joy'. But if they were to reflect for a moment on exactly what they were creating and feeling, the tears would be seen as relief from an accumulated tension around child birth, a relief that everything has turned out OK. Relief from tension, which means a freedom from fear. And that's not true joy, it is dependency on an external event for a sense of relief that is confused with happiness. But sometimes it is true joy, as joy is essentially life celebrating life, and the birth of a new human being is most definitely a time for life to celebrate life. But there are no tears in that joy, just a big warm glow on the inside, a big bright sunshining smile on the outside, and a radiant energy that 'infects' all whom it touches!

seen through and dissolved, can the bliss of real freedom return. In truth you are never not free, the prison and its bars are simply illusions that you mistake for reality.

Once you see when, and how, you are doing this, you will laugh, and your laughter will be the sign that you have seen through the illusion, you have corrected your mistake, and your spirit, which is you, will soar once again.

So YOU Are Still Unhappy

One of the most common ways in which you sustain your unhappiness, without being aware that you do so, is because you sustain the belief that you have to go somewhere and get something, do something or meet someone, or be somewhere away from here, where you always are.

You may have noticed this is a recurring theme of this book and the red thread that runs through and behind all the ideas and insights that you find here. Lets tug that thread again!

Unknowingly you keep trying to break a natural law of life. It's a law that says you are always present 'here', and you can never go or be anywhere else!

Your body can travel to what appears to be far flung places. Your words can be sent to the furthest corners of a cornerless world. But you are always right HERE. Right here and right now. Have you not noticed yet?

Even when your body travels, you are still 'here', there is no 'there' in the reality of you. Only here. As long as you believe there is 'a there' you will be discontent, which means unhappy, and therefore always searching for happiness some 'where' other than 'here', in a place called 'somewhere', which is 'nowhere'!

Only when you remember there is no 'where' can you be 'now here'. Welcome home to 'here' where you always were and always will 'be'.

Staying 'here', where you always are, is obviously not so easy as we have developed strong inclinations to try to be somewhere else. What may help is a clearer insight into what is 'really going on' within your consciousness, within you, within the self, when you attempt to go somewhere that you cannot be!

To develop this clarity, believe it or not, it's useful to go to the movies!

Lets go see a movie.

That's Extremely Offensive!

One of the most popular and frequent ways that we kill our own happiness is when we decide to be offended. Do you ever take offence at what someone says or does? Do you ever feel insulted and become upset as a result? I'm sure you can see where this is going. It's coming right back to you! If you feel offended it means you are emotionally disturbed. And who creates the disturbance? Not them. You do! Why? Ego! It's because you have created, attached to and identified with an image in your mind that does not concur with the 'others perception' that you then believe 'you' have been offended. If someone says to you, "You are a stupid fool" and you feel insulted or upset at their words, it's because you are attached to an image of your self being seen as a bright, highly intelligent and perfect person. If you were not attached to and identifying with that self-created self-image you would not be upset/offended and you would not respond emotionally, you would not kill your own contentment. You might say instead, "That's interesting, I haven't had that feedback before!" Or you could say, "Well that's your opinion, your perception, to which you are entitled." If everyone realized and understood this dynamic, almost all the conflict in the world would disappear. Unfortunately in some cultures it takes very small things to 'trigger' the belief that "I am offended by you," and the consequent emotional pain that follows. Some peoples ego is quick to anger and attack back. We only 'take offence' because we don't know our self. And it's that ignorance that is the root of all forms of the insanity that we call conflict, regardless of whether it's between two people or two nations.

Going to the Movies

Do you remember the cinemas of yesteryear? The original cinemas were usually large impressive halls. Sometimes converted town halls. Their most prominent features were the high-ceilinged spaciousness, the elegant décor and the balcony. Some decades ago, going to the cinema was a special treat. And in those more innocent days the movie still had the power to invoke a sense of awe and wonder, of excited expectation, and the privilege of entering another universe and visiting other worlds.

Come with me now to the cinema. You arrive in a soft and embracing seat. The lights are still up. You are aware of the spaciousness of the auditorium. There is also a library-like hush in the atmosphere, as people trickle in. It is this spaciousness, and an almost reverent silence, occasionally broken by soft whispers in the background, that fills your awareness as you quietly and expectantly await the start of the movie.

As the lights gently fade to darkness, somewhere above and behind you there's a click and a clack and a clackety-clack, as the projector gets going in the tiny booth buried behind the wall at the back of the auditorium. Suddenly multi-coloured images start dancing across the screen in front of you. The magic of another sound and vision show is under-way. Slowly your awareness loses its spaciousness. Your attention has narrowed to become exclusively devoted to the flickering images on the screen. As the story begins, the most colourful characters are introduced and developed. It's not long before your awareness and your attention have not only lost their spaciousness but they have left the original location in your body and are now in the movie. You are becoming personally involved in the story, as you start to lose your 'self' in the the plot. You know this because certain emotions begin begging for your attention to 'feel' them. Excitement, fear, disbelief, foreboding and frustration are only a few.

It's not long before you are almost totally absorbed by the events on the screen. You are going through what one, and sometimes several, of the characters are going through. Their trials, tribulations and tests become yours. Their emotional reactions become yours. Their enemies become your enemies. You live vicariously through the characters. You have been 'sucked in'. It might as well be you that's up there on the screen. And sometimes it feels like you are.

The story builds to a climax and you let it take you with it. Sometimes you are on the edge of your seat with tension, and at other moments you slump back in relief. Sometimes you are laughing out loud and at other moments you feel like weeping. The story ends and Hollywood has done its job. You are sighing or crying, enthusing or confusing your self, trying to work out what and why and who and how and wow!... wasn't that just great!

Up come the lights and the reality of where you are sets in with a thud. But of course the movie is still playing in your head, the emotions are still washing through your mind, though somewhat fainter. The flavour of the story is still present in your thoughts and feelings. As you return to the cold night air you don't feel it as you are still in the movies' aura. You are still living in the story, still reaching inside to feel those emotions again. This can last for a few hours or even into the next day, depending on how absorbed you were, depending to what extent you got sucked into the plot, into the characters. Next days cappuccino conversations were then filled with 'did you see'...'wasn't that amazing'... 'I wish I could be like that'..I am definitely going to see it again'.

Eventually the images and the emotions of the plot and characters fade into the background of your memory as the story is lost in your subconscious.

Reflecting on Projecting

If you take a moment to reflect you will see what really happens within you when you watch a movie. The source of the light and of the dancing images on the screen was above and behind you in the form of a projector containing a powerful light and some prerecorded film. It was not long before you gave the status of reality to the projected images on the screen as you convinced yourself that what you were watching was really happening. You became so absorbed by those images, giving them such deep meaning, that you surrendered your self, and therefore your mind and intellect, to the story. You allowed the story to shape your thoughts and feelings and at times you rendered yourself helpless. You were deeply impressed.

In other words the projected images, that you took into yourself, were allowed to make a deep impression far into your consciousness. That impression absorbed 'your' light and sucked up your energy, you. And what was obviously unreal up there on that screen, became real for you in your consciousness. You made the unreal real.

The whole experience is a metaphor for an 'insperience' you will create countless times every day. So let's go to the real cinema, the auditorium of your consciousness, where the screen is the screen of your mind, you are the script writer, the director, the projector and, all too frequently all the actors on the screen!

The Auditorium of Being

Let's say you have learned to meditate and you are now a master of meditation. Through gradual practice, you have mastered the art of letting everything come to an absolute rest within you. Like one of those rare summer evenings where there is absolute stillness in the natural world that surrounds you. Nothing is moving, not even a light breeze, it's almost eerie. You cannot help but notice the silence, you cannot help being moved by the stillness. As a master meditator, you are able to bring all feelings, memories, experiences, urges, desires, impulses to a point of utter stillness and silence within your self, within your consciousness. Let's say you have mastered that art.

You are now sitting in the auditorium of your being, the cinema of your consciousness... aware of the immense spaciousness of your being... aware of the vast timelessness of your being... aware of the complete stillness of your being. It's a kind of inner awe but you're not thinking, "Wow this is awesome!" You are just aware of a profound stillness, a powerful silence, and a deep sense of the unlimitedness and unendingness of ...you. You feel light, and you are also aware that 'light' is what you are.

OK so here we go, the movie is about to start. Up until this point your attention is unfocused, your awareness is unbounded spaciousness. Suddenly your attention is caught by a story that is starting to appear on the screen of your mind. Your inner stillness is broken by a series of memories that are being projected by a light somewhere behind you. Not behind your body, but behind you.

That light is you. At that moment you are not aware that you are the light that is projecting itself through a prerecorded 'film' of images called memory. But your attention is caught by what is appearing on the screen of your mind. For a moment you think a thought of recognition, "Oh it's the holiday row with David/Mary." but before you can catch your self and realize it's just an old and useless memory, you start to watch the story playing out as if it's real. You become so lost in the projected images of these memories that you feel as if it's happening right now. You start to recreate and feel certain emotions, the emotions that you felt when the argument actually happened all those months ago.

You begin to live in the scenes that you are projecting onto the screen of your mind. Your attention is absorbed by the scenes which means you are absorbed in the scenes on your mind. You lose your self in the a story that is unfolding before you, within you. You are at the movies in the auditorium of your consciousness. This can last for a few seconds or a few minutes.

Something or someone outside may distract your attention, and suddenly you will come out of the story and give your attention to that something that appears to be happing outside of you. But even then, you may start to notice that the event outside is really happening inside, on the screen of your mind. You bring the outside inside through your perception and you recreate it, interpret it, according to your 'state' of consciousness, and then project it up onto the screen of your mind, all in what seems like the same moment.

Once the distraction has passed, you return to the David/Mary story. After a few minutes of living the argument again, one small but powerful thought about the argument slips, like a subtitle, onto the screen, "It's past. It's gone. Can't change it now." And suddenly you are back in your seat in the centre of your self, in the auditorium of your consciousness, a little shaken, a little unrelaxed, perhaps a little relieved … it's not actually happening now. And as you reflect for a moment you realize it did just happen again now, because you made it happen now, you recreated it, and projected it, and lost your self in it, just then, in your mind, on the screen of your mind.

As you 'reflect' upon what just happened 'in here' within your consciousness, the metaphor completes itself. The projector is your consciousness, the light is the light of your awareness/attention, the film is your memories and the screen is the mind, your mind. And the eye you watch it all through was the eye of your intellect, but it was only partially open because you lost your self in the story that you were projecting, just as you did in the cinema. And you lost the awareness that it was YOU that was projecting. It's as if you left the centre of you and went to live in your mind. You allowed your self to be trapped in the images that you were creating and projecting onto the screen of your mind. And, as we saw earlier, this is the mistake that gives birth to ego – the false sense of 'I'. Can you see it? Did you notice it? This is how you attempt to separate your self from your self, many times every day.

Can you see how easy it is to lose your self in the movies that you create, in the stories, in the images, that you project onto the screen of your mind? In fact we are all doing this almost all our waking time. We live our life through stories, filled with fictional characters that we create for ourselves about ourselves and others. Go and see seven different movies on seven nights at your local cinema and each night you will lose your self in, and identify with, the characters in each movie. After a week, you will either be tired of going to the movies, because it's tiring to keep shifting your identity from character to character, or you will become thoroughly addicted, because the characters live excited, over-stimulated and seemingly significant lives, and so you do too, for a couple of hours at least.

Take a moment to reflect, how many movies, how many stories, do you run in the auditorium of your being during your average week, your average day? Probably a lot more than seven, probably more like seventy. And in each little story, there is a character called 'me'. Yes some versions of me are similar, and seem to have continuity across stories, like a series of episodes of The Life of Me. But many characters of 'me' can seem quite different. And every time you tell one of these stories about 'me', your old friend, the ego, is celebrating a new life, a new character, a new identity. Remember, the definition of ego is attachment to and identification with the wrong image of my self or belief about my self. And that's why you can be sure that most stories will contain some kind of suffering. At the very least that suffering will be at the end of a story, the end of the movie...until you run it again.

We all learn to lose our self in characters that we create about our self. But they are simply images, beliefs about a self that is not you. The real you, the true you, is not an image on the screen of your mind, it's not a conceptualized character in a story. You are the creator, you are the light of the projector, you are the light that illuminates the characters in your stories, that shines through the film of memory and lands on the screen of your mind as multi-coloured characters in their own little dramas. They are your creation, and you are the creator. And the creator is not the creation. The illuminator is not the illuminated. But the moment you lose that awareness, the moment the illuminator believes it is the illuminated, the ego is born, the mistake is made... and it's all downhill from there.

What else happens when the light, the illuminator (you), confuses itself with the illuminated (characters in a story called my Life)? The illuminator (you) will feel finite, as the characters that you create and identify with are all limited. You feel time-bound because they are all living in a material context which constantly changes. You feel 'mortal' because all characters in a time-bound context fade and die in the end, unless you freeze frame, which is almost impossible in the auditorium of your consciousness. Unless you really are a 'master meditator'!

But the light of the illuminator, that's the real you, in reality is infinite, unlimited, timeless and immortal in its true essence. These are unimaginable concepts. They are imageless ideas. They are beyond the mind. They are prior to the mind. That's why it's impossible to identify your self with them. If you try, it's as if you are attempting to contradict them. A light bulb is at its brightest, with the capacity to illuminate a whole room, only when there is nothing surrounding it like a lampshade or objects like furniture. Similarly the light of your self, your consciousness, has the capacity to shine at its brightest only when there is nothing surrounding it, nothing absorbing it's light. In other words when you do not attach your self to anything or anyone, then you are at your brightest. When you don't lose your self in images on the screen of your mind that's when you feel most free, most powerful, most outgoing, most giving and most at peace with your self.

Unfortunately you spend your entire life learning to attach your heart, your self, to images of people, places, possessions. All of these images are created and recorded by consciousness, by you, etched on the film of your memory and then replayed on the screen of your mind. It's that screen that blocks the radiance of your light. It's on that screen that you get lost in fictional stories about you and your attachments. And as you fill the screen with characters and places, all finite and limited, it gives rise to feelings of limitation and finiteness. But you think it's real. You have been filming, projecting and attaching to the images of the characters you believe are you in your inner cinema, almost all your life, and you believe it is real.

You cannot see that this is not living, it is losing your life, which is your light, in an illusion of life. And then, when it all gets a bit tiring, when you exhaust your self with your illusions of reality, you pop out to the cinema to live in an illusion of an illusion.

What a wonderful life!

The Dance of the Seven Veils

There is a dance, which apparently originates somewhere in the Middle East, that memorializes the process of restoring the pure and unhindered light of consciousness. It is often remembered as the dance of the seven veils. During the performance of the dance, the dancer removes, one-by-one, each of seven veils, until they are naked. It is the ultimate striptease, but with the deepest spiritual symbology. Each veil represents a story that we tell ourselves about ourselves. It is a story that we project onto the screen of our mind. Then we hide behind and hide in the story as we identify with an imagined character within the story. We veil ourselves in these stories and thereby hide our nakedness, the naked light of our pure being. They are the main 'movies' that we play in the auditorium of our consciousness They capture and trap our light, and siphon off our power.

If there is such a thing as a spiritual journey from here to there, from where you are now to where you need to be, this is it. If there is a pilgrimage to the truth this is it. It is a pilgrimage of removal, a spiritual striptease, except it's no tease!

As you remove the seven veils, which means as you see through the unreality of the stories you have created and tell your self about your self, then you gradually reveal your self to your self. Except the one and only thing you can never see is your self!

Here is where the real dance of life takes place. You have spent your life, and probably several lives, dressing up, unable to see the connection between your suffering and the costumes that you wear which are the stories you tell your self about your self. For most of the time it's fun to dress up, to lose your self in exciting fictional tales and splendid emotional adventures. Until it all becomes too much, too intense, too emotionally painful, and you consciously search for a reason for your pain and conflict, a reason for the downs in life that seem to get longer and deeper as life goes on.

So here you are, as if you are standing at the threshold of a room which you cannot enter unless you are prepared to become completely naked. It is the 'undressing room'. There is no name on the door, only a small sign that says, 'The Liberation of the Self'. Only this time it's not the beginning of another story, it's the ending of all stories. As you will see the ego does not like it and so there will be, if there isn't already, some resistance.

The Seven Veils are the Seven Stories

Liberating your self from these stories requires a clear awareness of the story itself. This in turn requires some time in meditation or contemplation. Only then will you start to clearly see how you create the story and then lose your self in the story. Only then will you realise that 'it's just a story' and you are not a story! If you are tired of losing your self in fictional tales, if you are ready to come out of hiding and bring an ending to pretending, if you are ready to get undressed and liberate your self, here are the seven veils with accompanying meditation/reflection. Music and lights and …action!

The First Veil

The Story of Your BODY IMAGE

How is your body image? If you are not happy with your body image, which means if you have created and tell your self a negative story about your body, there is now an industry out there ready to nip it, tuck it, slim it, stretch it, shrink it, augment it, highlight it, dress it and, if it's just the two dimensional image you'd like to alter, airbrush it! In short these industries tell you a story about your body and encourage you to identify with the story and make it your story. You learn to believe that you are your body and that your body is inadequate as it is. They help you to affirm that your body image is not up to scratch, and that is why you are not feeling good about your self and about the world. Then they tell you how they can fix it. You believe them and so you begin to create your "I am a body' story, with a 'subplot' that keeps reminding you that your body image is inadequate and needs to be fixed.

From the day you arrive you are encouraged by the world around you to create your 'body image' story. You become convinced that you are only a physical form. Up on the screen of your mind, you replay the images of your form that you have seen hundreds of times in the mirror, and as time goes on, pressured by a media that presents only perfect bodies, you start to create an increasing number of judgments, many of which are negative, about your own body.

Seeing through this story called 'I am my body image' means realizing you are not your body, it's your vehicle, your dwelling place, your temple, your chariot, but it's not you. As you see how you mistake your self for the image of your body on the screen of your mind, you begin to loosen this 'veil' across your consciousness, across you. You begin to stop playing one of the many themes of this story which sounds like, "I look terrible therefore I feel terrible.' No, you don't look terrible because you now know that you cannot see your 'self' in a mirror.

As the veil of the image of your body slides off the screen of your mind and down to the floor of your consciousness your inner striptease is well under way!

Meditation/Contemplation
Sit quietly - relax - watch all thoughts that arise concerning your body - consciously create one thought *'I am not this body, I am the being of consciousness that dwells within, and animates this physical form'* - gently concentrate your attention around that thought - allow it take root -

simply watch any conflicting thoughts come and go - return to and animate this one thought - then let it go - be aware of your self being aware of your self as nothing more than the light of awareness - free of attachment to any thought about anything - even if it's just for a moment, with practice, that moment will expand and you will start to taste a new freedom. Be patient.

The Second Veil

The Story of Your PERSONALITY

What is personality? It is a tapestry of traits, tendencies and habits that you create and bring together within your consciousness and then play out through your thoughts, attitudes and actions. But your personality is not what you are, these tendencies/traits/habits are not what you are. You are the creator and they are your creation. It's just that they become fixtures in the auditorium of your being and you start to identify your self with them.

The journey through childhood is a time when many people project on to you their perception of your character, your personality. You believe them, recreate what they see, alongside what you see, and behave in ways that affirm their and your description of your personality. Over time certain character traits and tendencies seem to become permanent fixtures within your personality. You build a story around these traits, around the kind of person you see yourself as. You start to believe that you are that 'personality'. All around you the 'cult' of personality seems to affirm that the most important thing in life is to develop your personality. It 'seems' that you will not be successful in life unless you have ...personality.

Sometimes you articulate the kind of person that you believe you are as you share bits of your 'personality story' and say things like, "I am a worrier….. I always get upset... I just can't seem to understand... I am a slow learner… I always react to such people... it's my nature"! What you don't realize is that you are not talking about your self, you are simply talking about certain traits, habits and tendencies that you have developed. But they are not what you are.

As we reminded ourselves earlier, personality comes from the idea of 'persona', which means mask. We all learn how create a mask, and often many masks, and then hide our 'self' behind the mask. There will be different masks for different sets of traits and tendencies, which we then tend to 'wear' in different relationships. Then the masks become your identities, and around each identity, each mask, you create another story about your self.

To realize you are not your personality, that you are not the accumulated habits, traits and tendencies that you have created, is to see through the illusion upon which these stories are based. It is to take off the veil of your personality. A veil that in itself can have many layers. Now that may sound a bit scary and you may even think, "But surely, without a personality I would be nothing, I would be like a zombie, a clone, a non-entity". But the opposite is true. Your personality (traits/tendencies) is based largely on your attachment to certain beliefs, emotions and actions i.e. it is based on ego. When it is 'seen through', when the story is dropped, your true personality is revealed. The authentic you comes through. Only this time it's not a mask, it's not a veil, it's not a fictional tale about your self, that you are attempting to sustain.

What is revealed is the authentic peaceful, loving, joyful, unlimited and infinite you. The you that no longer needs to cling to and identify with any trait, habit or collection of tendencies. The you that no longer limits you to a set of reactions or certain behaviors. The you that has realised that you don't need to develop a certain personality just to 'fit in', or to please others, or to get others attention. It is the real you, the authentic you, the free you. But of course you cannot know this for sure until you are prepared to risk divesting your self of all that you have come to believe is you at the level of personality.

How do you know the difference between a story about you based on your personality and the true you? You know the story is personality based when your personality changes according to the circumstances or the person you are with. Whereas the real you is stable, ever positive, ever open, ever able to accept others as they are, in all relationships. You 'feel' the same in all situations and no longer hide or compromise your self in any relationship. And most crucially you no longer 'react' to anything or anyone, but you respond proactively to everything and everyone no matter what they have said or done. Regardless of what others say or do, you do not take it personally.

Meditation/Contemplation
Sit quietly - relax - replay a recent interaction with someone to whom you reacted emotionally - watch the story unfold on the screen of your mind - identify the behavioural trait or tendency that came to the forefront of your reaction - name it - look for the attachment behind the emotion - now replay the interaction in your mind but this time see yourself responding quite differently - calmly and coolly - peacefully and positively - practice this and you will start to notice you become less reactive in such situations and more aware in 'real' time - you will notice you are more your self. Be patient.

The Third Veil

The Story that is Your HISTORY

The presentation of your CV at the job interview, or as a document of your credibility, is the moment when you say, "Look at my qualifications, my experience, my achievements, this is me." But of course it's not you, it's just a story. It's just a history or a 'herstory'! A story of what you have done in the past. It's not what you are.

Just about every conversation with any new acquaintance will lapse into large chunks of what you believe to be you in terms of your history. You will tell the story of your life before this moment now, believing it to be a way of telling someone something about your self. But it's not who you are, or what you are, it's just a story. And you are not a story.

For most of us, our history is a powerful tale etched on the inner film called memory. It is one of our most popular movies, starring our self. We pull up and project your history onto the screen of our mind, and then take delight in turning it into words and broadcasting to whoever will listen. And every time we do, we strengthen the illusion that we are talking about our self! We don't see that we are simply veiling our self with another story.

Taking off this veil is not easy. It's become a kind of support, a tale into which some of us run and seem to find safe haven. Others are always trying to escape their past, still believing it is more real than the present, so they attempt to force it out of their awareness as it still has seems to have power over them. In doing so they only make the story stronger. But in reality the past is always just a bunch of memories and they have absolutely no power over you when you finally see through them, when you see that those memories are not what you are. This requires the initial practice of being *aware* of how you lose your self in a history of actions, and then *disassociating* your self from that history. Not suppressing the story, not denying the story, not fighting the story of past thoughts, feelings and actions, simply seeing and realising, "I am not this story. It's not me. It's just a record of some thoughts/feelings/actions, but it's not what 'I Am'. It's a series of images of previous events that I witnessed, but it's not me."

In truth, from a purely spiritual point of view, from a true point of viewing, 'you' have no past. Your actions, your creations, leave records in your memory and in the memories of others, but they are not what you are. Can you sense the freedom in this insight? This is not to say that we go around doing anything to anyone and then saying, "Well it's past now and I am not my past, so it was not me." This is to abdicate responsibility for your creation, for your actions now. All actions do have consequences. You are dealing today with the consequences of your actions yesterday. And the reason for that is your actions yesterday were not aligned to the truth in you, which means not aligned to what you truly are.

To remember and identify with any memory of action that you created yesterday is to identify with what you do. And as we saw earlier you are not what you do. What you do is not what you are. However if you create any action that is based on a false identity that you give yourself, then that action will live in your consciousness as incomplete, as unfinished business, because it was not created in alignment with the truth of who you are. This is why our ego based actions today come back and haunt us tomorrow; and why our ego based actions yesterday come back as haunt us today. Not just as they ripple out and return from the universe of our relationships 'out there', but also from the universe of our own consciousness or, to be more accurate, our conscience! This of course is the principle we sometimes call 'karma'.

The 'burden of our karma' is defined by all the actions that we created while in a state of ego i.e. attached to and identified with something that we are not, including our history. This is one of the reasons it takes so long to resolve our karma. One of our deepest attachments (misidentifications) is to the past. The quick way to resolution is to stop identifying with what you are not, and that includes no longer seeing your self in terms of your past. It's just a story and YOU are not a story.

Have you ever noticed how some people spend their life trying to live up to their past. There was, at some point, a major achievement for which they gained some recognition. Suddenly they had a story of glory about their self that they could grasp and identify with. The feelings (emotions) at the time were also powerful that they spend the rest of their life attempting to re-create this story and the emotions they felt at the time. Then there are those who spend their life attempting to create a 'distinguished past'. Their goal is to achieve something so great in the eyes of others so as to ensure they will be remembered, recognized and respected by others in 'retrospect'. Both are the work of the ego creating, replaying and attaching to a story about the self that is neither true or real.

Meditation/Contemplation

Sit quietly - relax- bring into your awareness an image of a one page profile of your life - on the profile is a brief summary of your past actions and achievements - allow it to catch fire at the base and then watch it gradually disappear in flames - be warmed by the flames - remind your self that freedom has no history - your past is now past and gone - feel how free you are now. Be patient.

The Fourth Veil

The Story of Your RELATIONSHIPS

The second and third veils i.e. the stories of personality and history, are intimately woven together with the fourth veil, the story of our relationships. The context of our life is dominated by our immediate relationships. Family, friends and colleagues are the main characters in a movie called My Relationships. Each relationship is different and each has its own story, its own plot. We create a self image central to the story of each relationship.

In some relationships, you may seem more relaxed, in others you are happier, and in some you seem to be regularly miserable. There is a slightly different story about who you are in each relationship. You create and identify your self with a different the image/idea of the character that you see your self as in each relationship. It is then easy to feel fragmented and sometimes confused. Deep down, you don't really understand why you seem to be a slightly different person (sometimes not so slightly) with different people. Why can't you just be the same, consistent, always relaxed, contented, easy-going you?

Then there is the history of each relationship. Some of those histories, especially within our family, go back a long way. Some we like to talk about with great frequency with friends and colleagues, and others we only talk about to ourselves in our own heads, as we tell and retell our historical stories with some people more than others. We lose our 'self' in the stories, get stuck replaying them and completely identify our self with our roles within them.

There is of course a high degree of attachment to our relational histories, which is why we keep remembering them. Hence the often intense emotional content that is woven through each one. It's not wrong and it's not bad, but what we don't notice is that as long as we attach to and identify with our relationship stories we are not able to give, to share, true love within those relationships now. We find it hard, and in some cases impossible, to be our authentic self within those relationships. This is of course why families can easily become places not of sweetness and light, but trouble and strife.

The modern day portrayal of the creation and development of the dysfunctional relationship, and therefore troubled relationship story, is the TV soap opera. A group of characters co-create a drama out of a series of relationships, filled with intense emotions that drive conflict, blame, jealousy and the victim mentality. This is then perceived to be the natural, normal and the correct way to live. Such relationship stories filled with personality clashes and drawing on long histories even become 'news items' and are reported on as if they were real life relationships! Within such stories there is little if any authentic happiness, otherwise the plot would be flat and boring, and there is little if any true love, otherwise the relationships would be harmonious and largely uneventful to an external observer. We then measure our own life against such a diet of dramas, whether in soaps or movies. It's not difficult to start to think that our life isn't interesting and worthwhile unless we too are involved in such emotional too-ings anf fro-ings with those around us.

Little do we realise that in the process of creating lots of little dramas with those who are apparently close to us we are sabotaging our peace, suppressing our capacity to love and strangling our own contentment and joy.

When there is any agitation or pain in any relationship you start to create memories and formulate a story of that encounter, of those 'emotional moments'. Slowly but surely you attach to and identify with these memories and whenever you meet or think about that person those memories resurface in your mind to dominate your thoughts and feelings

So many stories with so many people. You run in and out of stories in your mind, playing each story on the screen of your mind one minute, and then growing the story in the film archives of your memory the next. But they are just stories and they have no basis in reality. They might as well be one of those fairy tales you were told by a parent as they lulled you to sleep. They are your very own soap operas running in the cinema of your being. So long as you keep playing them you keep yourself asleep to your authentic self. Ultimately it is these stories that stop you meeting people fresh and new, without what is sometimes referred to as baggage from the past. Baggage is just the story of the beliefs that you have created about the other 'yesterday' and every time you see them 'today' you tend to affirm and strengthen your attachment to those beliefs.

Then you wonder why you sometimes find it hard to connect with certain people in your life. In truth you are often connecting more to your beliefs, your story, about the other, than to the person themselves. Which is why it has been said that in any meeting between two people six people turn up! There is the story of how you believe others see you, the story how you would like others to see you and the story of how you actually are. Then there the story of how 'they' believe others see them, how they would like others to see them and how they actually are. So many stories gather for one meeting! No wonder relationships can be...challenging! Even Hollywood isn't that busy!

The veils of your relational histories are some of the hardest veils to shake off. So much of our 'self', our identity, seems to have been invested in them. We are so attached to our stories that to let them go, to detach, to realise past is past, to see that each story is largely a set of 'emotional memories' that have no value in the present moment, is not so easy. To see our relational stories as little more than mental prisons is not as easy as visiting your grannies house for tea and scones and a good chat about the ...family history!

But if you are to be a free spirit again, if you are to liberate your capacity to meet life with a fresh, enthusiastic and renewable energy, the veil of our relationship stories has to go, it has to be stripped off, otherwise you just get stuck in storyboards full of judgment, blame, regret, guilt and shame and such thoughts as, "I remember when you/they made me feel...I am never going to forget what did to me...wasn't that awful what happened to us twenty years ago". Even the 'good memory' stories are veils that obscure the real you and keep you trapped in relational histories. All memories are like photo album. You don't get up in the morning and spend the day in the photo album. Yesterday, even if it was filled with good feelings, cannot be recaptured or repeated. Attempting to do so is like eating stale bread.

Meditation/Contemplation

Sit quietly - relax- take a moment to recall one of the people that you consider closest to you - bring their image up on the screen of your mind - allow the history of that relationship to run it's story..a little - watch the story - then stop the story - see only them in your mind - allow the image of their face to fade to a point of radiant light - then allow all the memories and images of your story with them to be sucked into that point of light just as black hole sucks in all surround light into itself - so all there is left is a beautiful, shinning, radiant light - remind your self that this is their true form and it is also your true form - you are both free of all that has gone before - feel the freedom and the beauty of this 'real' connection that you now have with them - light intertwined with light - practise this visualisation and notice the difference it makes to your capacity to be your true self in their company. Be patient.

The Fifth Veil

The Story of EMOTION

We explored earlier how the root cause of all emotion is ego and how the ego is simply a mistake. So emotions are also mistakes. But they are powerful mistakes which 'kick up' large amounts of 'dust' in our consciousness. They are disturbances that can range from what feels like a small ripple to a huge hurricane. And when they happen, they often seem to be enlivening. Anger and fear create cortisol and adrenaline in our bodies and, while these chemicals are coursing through our body, we feel alert, attentive, awake and alive. We even cry in order to release our self from certain emotional pressures and suddenly sadness 'seems' to feel good!

These emotions not only become regular visitors to our daily life, they also become addictions. If our daily experience does not feature some 'drama', which is some form or face of anger, fear or sadness, then it feels like something is missing from the day. It feels like there was and is an emptiness. Nothing much happened. Emotion didn't happen. So some days we go looking for reasons to be offended ("How dare you say that to me...") and we consciously ensure that we are in the company of someone that we know will press our buttons and we encourage them to do so, either consciously or subconsciously. We seek news at which we can be shocked and feel bereft ("Did you see that, wasn't it just terrible..."). We don't look for reasons to be cheerful but reasons to be sad and angry and scared. ("I am so frightened something horrible might happen…")

We build our stories of emotion as we record memories of our self feeling certain emotions. Then we invest our identity in those emotional stories. In attempting to affirm our 'emotional identity' we look for ways to live out those stories every day, believing them to be normal, and that we are being consistent with our 'emotional self'. Emotional addiction is the driver as we look for the chance to play a bit part in some daily scene, wearing the veil of our emotional story. We justify our emotional reaction and behaviour with, "Well I was just trying to help…I can see you need support and I'm just as angry as you are" But deep down we are just running our story so that we can 'feel those emotions' again and thereby affirm an emotional identity which is not what we are.

Again it's not an easy veil to drop, not an easy story to stop telling our self. Withdrawal symptoms will be apparent until the real emotionless (egoless) self is revealed and realized behind the veil. Only then is emotion seen for what it is. Like a mist in the early morning, it has no substance and no real power and, as soon as the sun comes up it is burnt away, it evaporates. As soon as the light, that is the true consciousness of the authentic self re-emerges, the fog and mists of emotion evaporate. Only then can you be at peace again. Only then can you choose your feelings again. Only then can you be a source of love in life…again.

If this is still not clear, reflect on Part II again. It takes time to see with absolute clarity how we create our emotions within our consciousness. When you fully see and realize with your real eye, the eye of your intellect, that you are not your emotions, and of course the love is not an emotion, you will have begun to take off the veil of emotion. But only to reveal an even subtler veil beneath!

Meditation/Contemplation
Sit quietly - relax - consciously create the emotion of fear as worry - feel it fully - then consciously create the emotion of anger as irritation - feel it fully - then consciously create the emotion of sadness as melancholy - feel it fully - then stop creating anything - allow all emotion to become

quiet - feel the quietness grow within - feel that quietness fully - feel the peace, the calm, the absolute tranquillity of that quietness expand - make this peaceful quietness a gift - give it as a gift to someone you know is a little peaceless - give them this gift with love - feel your peace and feel your love...fully - notice the solidity of these feelings - notice that what you are feeling is what you are naturally. Practice this with much patience.

The Sixth Veil

The Story of BELIEF

Belief stories about others are only the tip of iceberg of all the 'belief stories' that we carry in our consciousness. "Well do you know what I believe?…." Is often the most common introduction by someone who is about to tell you a story about their beliefs. While most of your beliefs are buried in your subconscious, recorded sometime and somewhere in the past, your belief system stories are most easily noticed when you talk and interact with others. Your belief systems are like computer programs that were installed in the hardware of your consciousness at an early age. And you have been affirming them, and updating them, ever since.

Not only do they emerge in your conversations, but you will live in them and identify with them, so frequently that eventually you will only feel comfortable with people who share similar beliefs stories. In fact you may be so attached to and identified with these assimilated and sustained beliefs that you may even become violent towards others who don't share them, don't understand them, or who simply have beliefs that seem threatening to yours. The news media reports every day on such clashes of belief system stories. There is no such thing as a clash of civilizations, only belief system conflicts. There is no such thing as a war of words, only a war of beliefs.

I am a Christian, I am a Hindu, I am a Muslim, are just the 'cover titles' of stories based on belief systems many of us have been programmed with, usually at an early age. We learned to project these stories up on the screen of our mind and then to create characters called, 'I am a Christian' or 'I am a Muslim' as an image in our mind. We look at the image, the belief, and then say, "That's Me!" No it isn't, it's just a story. It's almost the same as watching the hero in the movie in the cinema and saying, "That's me up there!" No it's not, it's the story of a fictional and illusory character

To identify with any belief system is to create a fake story about your self based on a set of fallacious beliefs. It can only generate tension, defensiveness, worry, conflict and perhaps eventually hate. Give it up. Drop the story. Take off the veil. You don't need beliefs. To say I don't believe in anything is not to be a wimp, it's not a sign of weakness to have no opinion. In fact it's empowering because your power ceases to be drained in sustaining or defending your beliefs and their stories.

But it takes courage to let go of the belief that you need to have belief and to experiment with living beyond belief! It takes courage to give up believing and to cease identifying with and defending your belief stories. Why? Because, when you do you open your self to becoming aware of 'the truth' which can only occur in this moment now. Only when you lay yourself bare and make your self vulnerable to the truth, only then can you realize the deepest truth that nothing can touch YOU. You only need a 'defence system' when you hold on to and identify with your learned and assimilated beliefs. And where you create a defence system, you generate fear, anger and sadness, and therefore suffering.

For example, lets say that one day you decide to drop the story defined by the belief that others can hurt you with their insults or with the withdrawal of their approval or by their disrespect towards you. When you take the risk of dropping such a belief then instead of all your energy and attention being spent on blaming them for what your are feeling, and defending your self against their words, you are now free.

In that freedom you are able to look and see the real cause of your suffering was not coming from them it was coming from you. Why? Because you believed you were hurtable and insultable, you believed they should not shout, you believed that they should not be nasty, you believed that the world should be exactly the way you want it to be, and you believed that only then could you be happy. You believed the world should be perfect at every moment according to your belief about what a perfect world is. You believed that they and the world are responsible for your happiness.

As we near the end of the book perhaps it's becoming clear that such belief stories are not the truth. That's why it is highly recommend you get rid of them all. Strip them all away. Unless of course you wish to live in a prison of your own making for the rest of your life. Believe nothing, not even a word in this book. But don't start to believe that you shouldn't believe! Only when you cease grasping and defining your self according to a belief or a set of beliefs will you be able to 'see' what is real, what is true, for your self. Which really means being your authentic self.

Only then will you realize that you cannot actually see your self, that you are the seer of the seen. And the only thing the seer cannot see is the seer. That means all that you can see is not you. In that moment you will stop identifying with what you see, including your beliefs, and you will be free. You will have taken off the veil of belief.

Meditation/Contemplation
Sit quietly - relax - meditate and reflect on one question - what would you think and say if you had no beliefs - hold this question up to the light of your awareness - observe what occurs - play with the question - be open to whatever arises within you in response - sense the deep calm you might feel within your being when you no longer need to broadcast any belief.

The Seventh Veil

The Story of SUBTLE SELF IMAGE

After a lifetime of identifying with what you see in the bathroom mirror every morning it's no small challenge to realise and affirm you are not form but consciousness, not matter but light, not body but soul. To drop all the other 'I am' stories (I am what I do/I am where

I come from/I am what I have etc.) will not happen overnight, and certainly not with just one read of this book. It's yet another challenge to maintain the awareness of your authentic self as you navigate through your average day. But there is another self image that we are all just as deeply attached to and around which we are continuously creating fictional tales about 'me'. It is known as our 'subtle self-image'. It's the hardest story to see and the hardest veil to take off. It's a mixture of history, relationship and belief. It lingers somewhere in the background of your consciousness, fading in and out of your awareness, like a ghost on a foggy night, until that penny really drops around what we really are, not in theory, but for real.

The story of your subtle self image is usually the first gift from parents, teachers and siblings, as they pass judgment on you at a very young age. When people say things like, "You can't...you're not very good...you'll never...you're just not up to it...you're a naughty little"... You take them at their word, absorb their words, and start to build the story of your subtle self-image. It doesn't matter if it's negative or positive, neither is true. No-one can know you as you truly are, only you can do that. But you won't be able to fully free your self from the story based on your subtle self-image as long as your subconscious continues to cling to the images of you that you received from others and continues to build and sustain the 'story of me' out of those images. All the positive thinking in the world will not help as long as you keep running that story.

Stripping your self of this veil requires two things, awareness and realization. First, awareness of your attachment to, and repetition of, this story in your thoughts and words. And then realisation, which means seeing that the real 'I' is the 'I' that says 'I am' behind and prior to this story. This is why some form of meditation or self contemplation is essential as a daily practice. It's only in this practice that self awareness deepens and realisation happens. Many people try to remedy the negative thoughts and feelings, that tend to arise from this self image, with 'positive thinking.' But it seldom works other than at a superficial level. The attachment to and identification with this subtle self image is prior to all your thoughts and therefore has a powerful influence on your thinking.

In the beginning, as you practice your meditative and contemplative exercises, you are likely to only get glimpses of being the 'I' free of any attachment to any image. Like the fog clearing for a moment and you 'see' far out to sea, then it closes and obscures your view again. So too there are glimpses through the fog of all your stories, depending on your level of self awareness and your courage to discard your veils. Like dressing and undressing and dressing again, you will become aware of your self as the 'light of awareness', which means the transparent and open you, the honest and fearless you, for a moment, until, by force of habit, you cover your self, you hide your light again, you become veiled by and lost in all your stories once again.

And then one day, one fateful, destined day, the fog is gone, burnt off by the blazing light that is the true you, the real 'I'. All your stories are clearly seen for what they are, just stories, and you are not a story. The veils are gone, incinerated by the light of pure consciousness, the pure you. The real, the true, the authentic you, is 'unveiled'. Only then are you are able to say with absolute, unshakeable conviction, "I stand naked before you". Which is good if for no other reason than you came naked, and you will have to leave naked!

In between there is always a choice, which is to live in an endarkened world called 'emotional suffering', or to live an 'enlightened life', which is living in the light of love.

In Summary

When you 'unveil your self' you 'dust off' all your attachments. In the process of noticing all the various ways that you cloak your self you have realized and now know:

Ego is formed the moment you attach your self, your heart, to anything, where 'thing' (object, idea, person, belief, memory) is simply an image · on the screen of your mind. That's where you 'misidentify' your self. You mistake your self for what is on your mind. And when something happens to that 'thing' it's as if it happens to you.

Emotion originates as a disturbance within your consciousness when the object of attachment and misidentification is damaged, threatened, moved or lost. Emotion will generally arise in one of three forms – sadness, anger or fear.

Love is not an emotion, it is a state of being within which there is an awareness of a connection with 'the all' without attachment to any 'thing' within the all.

Fear is love distorted by attachment. You create fear when you attach your heart, your self, to some thing, thereby distorting the pure, radiant light of the self, which is love, into the vibration of fear. Same energy, different vibration.

All emotion dies under observation. In the process of observing the emotion you detach from it and return to the centre of your self, where you always find your peace which is your power.

Feeling is something that you do, not something that just happens to you. To feel is to touch and perceive, and as human beings we can 'feel/touch/perceive' at three levels – physical, intellectual and spiritual.

When you are emotional you cannot choose your feelings. You have temporarily lost mastery of your consciousness.

To 'feel' true love it is necessary to give it, which means give of your self. And in whatever way you give, extend, connect, without any desire for anything in return, so you will 'feel' that love on the way out.

The auditorium of your being is where you bring the world 'out there' in 'here'. You then create, direct and project it according to your previous experiences of the world and learned beliefs about the world. This is how you create and sustain your 'stories' about the world and then attach to, identify with and hide in those stories. Love is then hidden and ego stalks the world.

YOU are ONE and the SAME

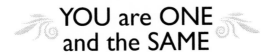

The Authentic **SELF** is what you are
when all in-authenticity has gone

A 'being' of **CONSCIOUSNESS** is what you are
prior to all that you 'do'

An individual **SOUL** is not something lurking
somewhere in your body, it's what you are

Radiant **SPIRIT** is not some mysterious energy
cruising through the universe, it's what you are

Pure **AWARENESS** is what you are
when there is an end to all attachment

The '**I**' that says 'I am' is what you are when all
aspiration to be anything other than 'I' is no more

The light of **LOVE** is not found anywhere other than
where you are, because it is what you are

Appendix

Becoming Aware of the Presence of Ego

Ego can be traced as the cause of many types of behaviour…including:
1 Criticizing 2 Possessing 3 Complaining 4 Blaming 5 Resisting 6
Fragmenting 7 Envying 8 Self Limiting 9 Projecting 10 Doubting 11
Defending 12 Protecting 13 Condescending 14 Correcting 15 Escaping
16 Avoiding 17 Denying 18 Desiring 19 Judging 20 Worrying 21 Lying
22 Disliking 23 Liking 24 Disapproving 25 Competing 26 Fixing (others)
27 Controlling.

Behaviour	Example	Specific Fear	Identification/ Attachment (to an IMAGE in the mind)
1 Criticizing	*"I think your idea is terrible and it will never work"*	*I think my idea is better and I'm scared your idea will be accepted*	*Attachment to and identification with the image of my idea*
2 Possessing	*"I didn't like it when I saw you laughing and obviously having fun with that person at the party last night"*	*I'm scared you might like me less, or even leave me*	*Attachment to and identification with the image of that person*
3 Complaining	*"This soup is cold – how dare you give me cold soup"*	*Fear that I am going to have to eat cold soup Or fear that this perceived sign of disrespect might continue*	*Attachment to and identification with the bowl of hot soup or the image of being respected*

4 Blaming	"It's their fault the report was not done properly"	Fear that people might think it was my fault	Attachment to and identification with the image of being Mr Perfect
5 Self limiting	"I can't ski" (after falling down and hurting my leg aged 10, thirty years later someone says, "Come skiing" to which the reply is "I can't ski"	Fear of success. Fear of stepping out of the small self image of being a 'not skier'. Fear of being more today than I was yesterday	Attachment to and identification with a small self image of being a not skier
6 Correcting	"Now look, let me show you the right way because you have done it very badly because its the WRONG way"	Fear they will do it wrong again	Attachment to and identification with the image of the task being done the right way which is usually my way
7 Avoiding	"I can't come to the meeting tomorrow"	Fear of communicating in a group where I may lose the respect and approval of the others or fear that I might have to do something as a result of the meeting	Attachment to and identification with the image of the respect and approval of others. Attachment to the idea of free time or control over my time
8 Desiring	"I want a new home"	Fear that I will get stuck in this home and not rise up on the property ladder	Attachment to and identification with the image of myself as upwardly mobile in the eyes of others

9 Disliking	*"I don't like him at all"*	*Fear that he will repeat the behaviour that I (mistakenly) thought had made me feel bad*	*Attachment to and identification with the image of myself feeling good*
10 Competing	*"I have to be the winner at everything"*	*Fear of losing face/prestige*	*Attachment to and identification with the image of receiving the recognition, attention and applause of others*
11 Controlling	*"If you don't get that job done by 3.30pm MY way there will be negative consequences for you"*	*Fear of the person doing it their way or being late*	*Attachment to and identification with the image of the job being done my way and on time*
12 Envying	*"You want someone else's position and/or their lifestyle"*	*Fear of not been seen as successful*	*Attached to and identification with the image of being respected by others for success*
13 Projecting	*"Lets start a 'project' to make the world a better place"*	*Fear that things will get worse in the world or just stay the same which is bad*	*Attachment to and identification with the image of how I think the world should or could be or the attachment to the image of self being 'the saviour' of the world*
14 Doubting	*"I am just not sure what you say is true and is a good thing to do"*	*Fear that if I follow you advice it will be a disaster*	*Attachment to and identification with the image of staying safe*

15 Defending	"I believe you are attacking ME all the time"	Fear that you may feel hurt	Attachment to and identification with the image of being comfortable and unhurt
16 Escaping	Running away from an intimate relationship	Fear that it might reveal your weaknesses, that your less than perfect self may be exposed	Attachment to and identification with the image of being seen as a strong, infallible and integrated person
17 Lying	"It wasn't me that took the money"	Fear of being seen as guilty or bad if the truth came out	Attachment to and identification with the image of being a good honest person
18 Arguing	"I am right about this and you are wrong "	Fear that you may be proved wrong and be seen is stupid or fallible	Attachment to and identification with the image of being right

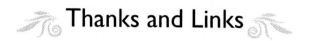

Thanks and Links

Thanks to all at the Global Retreat Centre for the silent space to see in the most powerful place to be - www.globalretreatcentre.com

Thanks to Bliss for the kind of music that relaxes heart and soul, and induces the occasional AHA! moment - www.blissfulmusic.com

Thanks to Marneta for showing us all how to reach the hearts of the children of the world - www.relaxkids.com

Thanks to the Brahma Kumaris World Spiritual University where anyone can receive free tuition in meditation in thousands of centres across 90 countries - www.bkwsu.org (Their books, CDs and DVDs are available at www.bkpublications.com)

Deep gratitude and buckets of love to all my sisters and brothers for your eternal and ever present subtle support

For more insights, workshops, retreats, seminars, talks, articles and meditations please see

www.mythsoflove.com and **www.relax7. com**

About the Author

Based in the Cotswolds in England, Mike 'plays' a variety of roles including author, spiritual teacher, coach, management tutor, mentor and facilitator.

In a unique blend of insight, wisdom and humour, Mike brings together the three key strands of 21st century - emotional/spiritual intelligence, management/leadership development and continuous 'unlearning'.

His previous books include:

Don't Get MAD Get Wise
The 7 AHA!s of Highly Enlightened Souls
In the Light of Meditation
Learn to Find Inner Peace
Learn to Relax
1001 Meditations
1001 Ways to Relax

Each year he leads regular awareness and enlightenment retreats throughout the world.

Mike can be contacted at mike@relax7.com and a schedule of some of his seminars, retreats and talks can be found at *www.relax7.com/diary*.

If you would like to subscribe free to Mike's *Clear Thinking* weekly e-article you can subscribe at www.relax7.com and then go to Room 1 – it's free.